Into HARMS WAY

Lieutenant Paul E Geidel
Rescue Company 1, FDNY, (ret)

Print ISBN: 978-1-48359-970-0

eBook ISBN: 978-1-48359-971-7

Cover photo by Gary Suson

FORWARD TO PAUL'S BOOK

The love of helping others is bigger than most of us can imagine. There are two groups of helping persons whom I admire the most: firefighters and war veterans. Whether a brave New York city firefighter or Korean War combat veteran, the more dangerous the situation, the more soaring is the mission!

Firefighters have a zest for life. Many have witnessed horrific events that most of us cannot imagine. Firefighters are the first to run into a building to help victims, as others are running out. Their heroism has been captured for decades by various media outlets.

Those that fought over 60 years ago in North Korea during the horrific war as gunners, have vivid images and somewhat clear recollections of what went on in the air during their night missions. The darker the night the more horrific the action. All those courageous vets who risked their lives for our country have a zest for life well beyond my capacity to understand!

This book is about a hero, my hero, my husband, Paul Geidel. Paul and I met in 1981 at a dimly lit crowded lounge in Woodbridge, New Jersey. He was retired for years from the Fire Department of New York City. Once we met, he talked about his career as a firefighter and veteran. Actually, the two hours we spent together were mostly about his fire fighting, which I found interesting.

Eventually we started dating. I came to realize just how much of a history Paul had during his life. Maybe because I was falling for him, or perhaps maturity set it, but I became interested in hearing his many stories about fire fighting, and the top flying aces from various wars!! Paul had turned me into an aviation buff!

Eventually, I introduced Paul to my parents. There was an immediate connection. Since Paul was almost fifteen years older than me, they were able to talk about what happened during "their day." Since my father served in the Army as military police during World War II, the conversations seemed to go on for hours. My mother appeared to enjoy the conversations as well. Paul never failed to bring my mother a hamburger from her favorite place whenever he visited which she devoured while listening to their conversations.

On the other hand, my three brothers, Mike, John and Bob, who were close in age to me, were taken back by the age difference, including Paul's grey hair. It was going to take time for me to convince them to overlook the age difference and focus on the man. However, it did not take too much time because they seemed to have much in common, sports, travel trailers, Harley riding, and family. Before I knew it, the grey hair became invisible! As for my sister, Cathy, she was fifteen years younger than me and just accepted him as her sister's new boyfriend.

Paul's mother and father were deceased. He was a divorced father of four grown children, Gary, Ralph, Michael, and Christine. Gary and Ralph were firefighters in New York City, Michael was working for a trucking company, waiting to be called for the fire department. Today, he is with Rescue I in Manhattan, New York. Christine is a brilliant scientist at a large pharmaceutical company. Their acceptance of me dating their father was with approval.

Paul was also very involved with fast-pitch softball. As a pitcher, he traveled to many beautiful areas of the country to pitch in tournaments. As a divorced mother of two children, James and Debbie, he often would take us to the tournaments. He was a great role model for my children. We all had a good time watching him pitch as well as fun touring such places as the Capitol Building in Washington, DC, the blue oceanfront waters of Ocean City, Maryland, the Corning Glass factory in Corning, New York to name three of the many places he played over the years.

For many years, Paul talked about writing a book about his experiences with the New York City Fire Department, Korean War and Fast-Pitch Softball. He did keep a journal of some stories as well as every newspaper article related to many of the events in which he was involved.

After putting a few firefighting, Korean War, and softball stories on Facebook, many of his followers encouraged him to write a book. The book you are about to read,...and at the same time is the culmination of Paul's writing efforts. His goal was to share his stories with others, those who love a good tale. In going through his book, even I learned more about my husband. I believe you will find his stories to be heartfelt and telling.

"INTO HARM'S WAY" BY PAUL E. GEIDEL

Forward by
Gary Marlon Suson
Honorary Battalion Chief, Fire Department of New York
Official Photographer at Ground Zero, FDNY
Founder: Ground Zero Museum Workshop

The world is full of everyday people who do larger than life things. Unfortunately, they are often overshadowed and overlooked in the news media by stories focused more on the sensational and the celebrity as opposed to the simple and sublime. Heroes arise out of unorthodox situations and events and only then do we take notice of their actions and special character. Firefighters are the epitome of bravery and loved by all - we stare at their trucks and sirens from childhood through old age in awe as they race down crowded city and suburban streets towards situations that everyone else runs away from - fires. Fire cares about no one - it steals lives every day and will continue burning and killing until it is stopped in its tracks. Firefighters are a unique breed - fearless - tough yet compassionate. When not in their rig, they spend hundreds of hours in their firehouses studying their nemesis like detectives searching for a murderer. Officers teach lower ranking members all the tricks of their trade and talk about fires of past. Hollywood has told some of their stories, portrayed their bravery and helped us share in their losses. On September 11, 2001, the world learned quickly about the bravery of firefighters, the dangers of their job and realization of their losses, as 343 of them were killed in 90 minutes - an unthinkable number. Whether Sitting around his firehouse dinner table during his 20-year-career as an FDNY Lieutenant or the many years after his retirement holding court with friends and other firemen in bars and social events, Paul E. Geidel has commanded the attention of all those lucky enough to hear his incredible stories from life in the FDNY in the 1950's, 60's and 70's, his adventures on a bomber in the Korean War and sadly his tough experiences with the September 11 attacks at the World Trade Center. Born August 8, 1933 - the same birthdate as his father, Paul Geidel's story began in Staten Island, New York. The son of a restaurant owner and a housewife, Paul learned about loss at a young age when his 1-year-old baby brother died of crib death. A practical joker with lots of energy at a young age, Paul quickly became bored after he graduated high school and enlisted in the U.S. Air Force at age 19. After his basic training in 1951, Paul went to gunnery school and scored the highest possible grade, a 4.0 and was quickly assigned to B-26 bombers at Langley Air Force Base in Virginia. After survival training in Reno, Nevada, Paul was sent to fight in the Korean War in October of 1952. His numerous bombing runs - mostly night sorties - were designed to stop the supply routes bringing ammunitions and food to supply the North Koreans on the 38th parallel as they attempted to spread communism to the South. Winning numerous citations and air medals for his distinguished flying career, Paul left Korea in April, 1953 with a total of 43 combat missions. Finishing out his Air Force career working on B-29 bombers in New Mexico and Wyoming, Paul finally went back to civilian life in 1955. Back in Staten Island, Paul overheard a guy one day talking about his studies for the exam to become a firefighter in the Fire Department of New York. After doing some research, he decided that would be a great career for himself and he too signed up for the exam. Unfortunately, 16,000 other men *also* thought it was a great idea and so the competition was fierce, especially seeing as only 300 new firemen were needed out of the 16,000 applicants. Paul went to school and studied hard for the test of which only 3,000 would pass. When the results came in, Paul was quite pleased to find out that he came in #25 on the exam in all of New York City and #1 in the borough of Staten Island. So began Paul's career in the FDNY starting February 1, 1957 and ending in November 1976. Throughout those years, Paul would become a Lieutenant and unwittingly graced many covers and feature stories in the New York Daily newspapers for his heroics in attempting to save lives. Known as a huge risk taker on dangerous fires, Paul would become known in fire department circles as "Crazy" Paul Geidel. Echoing that nickname, Paul was often quoted saying, "I always felt if you didn't get hurt just a little on the big fires, you didn't give it a hard enough try." Over the course of three decades, Paul collected all those news clippings and photos and even kept a detailed journal of notes that chronicled a vast array of fires and emergencies that his company was usually first on scene for as a member of the elite Rescue-1 firehouse on West 43rd street. Founded in 1915, Rescue-1 in Manhattan is known as the paramilitary of firehouses - the ultimate home to the finest and most revered firemen who work decades with the hopes of getting the call to join this legendary firehouse. Rescue-1 answers every call for the big jobs and are usually the first to arrive on scene. Priding himself on making it to the top firehouse in Manhattan, Paul was a commanding officer and worked daily to improve his knowledge of firefighting while acting as a teacher to the younger guys. In an unfortunate twist of fate, Paul's career was prematurely cut short in 1976 when he fell down a stairwell and injured himself during a call at the New York Times building. After his retirement, Paul would start a family in Tottenville, New York and have four children: a daughter Christine – who would later become an international pharmaceutical scientist and three boys, Gary, Ralph and Mike who would follow in their father's footsteps and become FDNY firefighters. Family life suited the fatherly nature of Paul, who also loved that his sons were all Eagle Scouts in the Boy Scouts of America and were involved in sports. He taught them everything he knew about firefighting and eventually they would become some of New York's Bravest with two of his sons - Gary and Mike - becoming firemen at Paul's Rescue-1 firehouse. Paul's love of firefighting and working in a firehouse was rivaled only by his deep love of fast-pitch softball of which he was a champion pitcher with a rise-ball that almost no one could hit. After extensive rehabilitation and teaching himself to pitch without putting a strain on his injured back and ankle, Paul eventually returned to the mound to play casually on a touring all-star softball team. Known as "un-hittable" - Paul would usually be teased and mocked by opposing teams who didn't know who Paul was when they suddenly saw this older man with an Elvis-like mop of thick white hair and a severe limp taking the mound. "Hey Grandpa!" they would scream at him until Paul began to pitch. As the taunts rolled in, Paul would shrug his shoulders and simply say, "I'm just an old man but I am still going to give it a try" with a cheeky laugh. One by one and with the flick of a wrist, Paul's famous rise-ball would bring the most arrogant of hitters to their knees in humiliation as they swung with all their might. As I write this forward, I do so with a smile on my face since I speak from experience as to what Paul could do with a softball. In 2002, Paul and his son Ralph Geidel - whom I dug with at Ground Zero - invited me to play in a softball game in Staten Island. They were a man short and said I could play if I wished. I knew nothing of Paul's history with a ball at the time and when I was warming up, I overheard someone say Paul was going to pitch. Paul was in his late sixties and limping around in pain so I couldn't help but giggle to myself and squint my eyebrows in amazement. Paul came walking by me in his uniform and looked down at me - "Gary, I need to warm up, you wanna catch a few for me?" I looked at him and said, "Aww, how cute, Grandpa is going to pitch?" Me and Paul loved to razz each other and this was a great opportunity to mess with him - I mean seriously, he is going to get up on that mound and pitch? Paul looked back at me and said, "Yeah, Grandpa is going to throw a few. Will you help an old man out and let me warm up with you?" I felt kind of bad there for a minute and obliged. He showed me where to squat down and Ralph threw me a glove. I had actually been a catcher and a pitcher in High School so this was all old hat for me; no big deal. As expected, Paul didn't have much of a wind-up with all his injuries - it was all arm and hand motion for him. His last words to me before he threw the ball was, "Now, Gary, keep an eye on the ball. Remember to watch the ball." I don't really recall the time between when the ball left his hand and when it reached my glove other than the ball broke hard right as it came in. It was that fast, however when it hit the leather like a freight train there was a large "smack" and the pain in my palm was excruciating. It went down into my forearm and I jumped up writhing in pain. As I cursed and threw the glove down, I clutched my forearm only to hear Ralph laughing and finally Paul belting out, "What's wrong buddy? Did Grandpa hurt you? How did Grandpa do? Did that hurt?" It is often said that the definition of insanity is doing the same thing over and over and expecting a different result. Paul said to me, "Come on, catch a few more for an old man. I will go easy." Whether it was pride or foolishness, I squatted back down on that fresh spring grass and caught one more and then I was officially done. My palm was throbbing and swollen as Paul giggled for hours. "You can't catch for an old man?" As he walked over he told me that I should be happy he didn't throw his famous rise-ball because if he had, it would have jumped up and broke my nose. However, I am way ahead of myself. How I met Paul Geidel was most unique and unorthodox. It was the end result of a tragedy and a weird twist of events in my life. I had become the Official Photographer at Ground Zero after the 9/11 attacks when the Manhattan Trustee of the Uniformed Firefighters Association - Rudy Sanfilippo - brought me in and asked me to document every area and aspect of the "Recovery Period" at Ground Zero so there would be a record of this period in history for future generations. I essentially lived at Ground Zero 19 hours per day and mostly kept to myself as I documented with my camera a vast array of events as they unfolded during the dig for the missing. Firemen were kind to me, taking me in as one of their own and looking out for me. Fate would eventually intervene and place me in front of the Geidel family.

I remember it very vividly, that freezing cold Winter night in January of 2002 at Ground Zero. I was 100 feet below ground level, deep in the "hole" at the former World Trade Center site looking for interesting artifacts to photograph. The WTC site was empty and it was around 9:00pm, when all the recovery workers were eating dinner up at the "Bubble" - the Salvation Army tent that served as a mess hall for 9/11 workers. Off in the distance I saw two men dressed in FDNY gear digging together in a corner made up of dirt, steel and rebar wire. I made my way over to investigate who the two men were and within minutes I learned their names: Ralph Geidel and his brother Michael Geidel. The two men were digging in the hopes of finding their missing brother Gary Geidel of FDNY Rescue-1, who died in the collapse of the World Trade Center Towers. On September 11, 2001, Gary Geidel had run down to the World Trade Center on his day off to help out and made the ultimate sacrifice while trying to save civilians from the burning towers.

The Geidel Brothers seemed just as curious about me as I was about them. Ralph was the more talkative one while Michael was standoffish and quiet. Michael stared at me as Ralph asked me who I was shooting photographs for. I explained that I was there on behalf of the Uniformed Firefighter's Association. Ralph proceeded to show me how to dig for the missing - what to look for and how to identify remains. He was fully committed to his work and in my opinion an expert on the "dig" at Ground Zero. Michael went back to digging as Ralph showed me the tools of his trade and made small talk with me. At one point I realized that these two men were special - their story was unique and they seemed heartfelt. As a historical photographer, I was drawn to the special stories and people who made up the *Recovery at Ground Zero* and I knew after five minutes that these two men and their story should be recorded. I asked them if I could shoot a quick portrait of them for historical purposes. Ralph obliged while the reclusive Michael shook his head 'no' and said he wanted no part of that. Ralph tried to persuade Michael with a sentence that is etched in my mind forever - "Come on Mike, let's do it for Gary." Mike said 'no' again, shaking his head and standing far away. Ralph told me to go ahead and just photograph him so I told Ralph how to stand and I was about to hit the trigger on my camera when Ralph turned to Michael and said, "Come on, Mike, please. For Gary..." Mike finally gave in and said, "Fine, ok, but quick - one photo." I was surprised that Mike agreed to be in the photo and when he stepped in to Ralph's left, I knew - as all photographers know - that I had an incredible image before I ever even pushed the button. I told them how to stand with their digging tools, even which feet to put forward and which feet behind and what to think of as I raised my camera. I told them to think about what their older brother Gary meant to them. That look in their eyes is something I would never forget. Ralph seemed to look right through me and my camera and out the back of my head while Michael's eyes began to glaze over, that watery film which precedes tears. It is good I nailed the image in just one frame because after Michael heard the camera winder advance he said, "okay that's it," and walked away. He was very emotional as any loving brother would be. It would become a historical image seen around the world and one that everyone could connect with - a modern day 'Saving Private Ryan' - brothers looking for a missing brother amidst a war zone in the middle of Manhattan. As me and Ralph became friendlier, he invited me to dig with him and his brother Mike - to hang out with them. Ralph took a liking to me and I instantly cared about these two guys as I could feel their pain and I respected their tenacity as they were at Ground Zero every day digging with their father Paul Geidel. "You need to meet my dad, he's around here somewhere," said Ralph. A quick scan around the site turned up no one. "He must be up at the bubble eating." Ralph went on to tell me all about his father, FDNY Lt. Paul Geidel, a Korean War veteran who had a long, storied career in the FDNY. "You'll meet him eventually," said Ralph. I had no idea at the time that not only would I meet Paul but that it would begin a 16-year friendship that I would truly cherish.

Days later, as I was hanging out with Ralph and Mike, Paul came over and I got to meet the father of the three FDNY firefighters. Paul was exactly as I expected him to be - old school and no nonsense. His dry, blunt sarcastic sense of humor was something that was great to be around. He had a joke and a wise crack every day and took no bunk from anyone. Aged 68 at the time, Paul and his sons would pick me up several times per week from my apartment in Manhattan in their old flat bed truck and we would all drive to Ground Zero to dig - and to photograph. Walking with a limp from his old back and ankle injury, Paul loved to talk about two things - fast-pitch softball and his glory days from the FDNY. He had so many stories - mostly sad and sometimes funny - from his years with the FDNY that it could have filled a book. His life was fascinating - despite the tragedy that had recently befallen his family with the loss of firefighter son Gary - and it was never a dull moment to spend time with him. At Ground Zero, he would pick a spot, sit down and dig. I admired him - what he had been through and the way he handled it all. As the dig at Ground Zero ended in May of 2002, so did the hope of Paul recovering any remains of his son. By then, I had become close with the Geidels and their pain was my pain - I was very sad that all they could do for Gary was have a memorial. I went to that memorial and watched the white doves get released as the tears around me flowed. So many families never recovered any of their loved one's remains at the World Trade Center site. Right as Ground Zero ended, I shot a portrait of Paul as well as a group image of Paul with sons Ralph and Michael. These are amongst my favorite in my vast collection because you can sense the bond of "family" when you look at these images. In Paul's portrait, you can clearly see the anger and emotions in his eyes which encapsulate the roughest period of his life: The loss of a son.

As the years rolled by, every so often Paul would share more and more stories both with myself and with his many friends on Facebook. I asked Paul why hadn't he done a book? These were unique stories from the New York City Fire Department chronicles - the greatest city in the world not to mention an incredible agency - the FDNY. I believed people on a grand scale would want to hear all these firefighting stories from the 50's, 60's and 70's in Manhattan on the front lines with firefighters. I was very pleased in 2014 to hear that Paul was indeed putting a book together and I was only too happy to have Paul use my images of him and his sons for the book. Tragedy befell the Geidel family again in October, 2014 when Ralph Geidel passed away unexpectedly of heart failure. As if Paul had not been tested enough in life – here he was again having to endure the loss of yet another son, this time as a result of illness derived from working 9 months straight at the WTC site. With dignity and courage, I watched Paul struggle through a tumultuous period of loss and in the process, he became one of my personal heroes. To say Paul Geidel is tough is an understatement - yet beneath that tough exterior lies a heart of gold and genuine care for others. I do not believe that Paul Geidel even realizes what he means to all of us that personally know him and are lucky enough to be called his "friend," nor is he aware of the positive impact he has had on our lives. This is quite common with down-to-earth people who do larger-than-life things. Paul falls under the category: Salt-of-the-earth. He represents the basic, fundamental goodness and honesty that the world has to offer via mankind. One of Paul's stories - "The Night I Wept" - is a great example of the emotional pains and fine print that come with being a firefighter. That story also represents - according to Paul - his greatest achievement as a firefighter. Paul's detailed stories will bring you into a time capsule and let you experience life on the front lines with him. His stories cross the gamut - from a young boy looking up at Paul and asking him if he will ever play basketball again after a horrible wooden escalator accident at Stern's Department Store to Paul's last ditch efforts to run into a smoke-filled building in a desperate attempt to save two little girls. These stories will leave you with a tear in your eye and a whole new appreciation for the life of a New York firefighter seen through the eyes of one man during a life that was spent committed to helping others. It has been a life well-spent. For me it is nice to finally see these stories arise from the firehouse dinner table and years of bar conversations into a beautiful book that everyone can now own. I am very honored to have been asked to be a part of this book in some small way. The portrait of Paul I shot in 2002 that is used for this book is as raw as it gets; I photographed it just after the Ground Zero Recovery came to an end. The emotions on his face are unfiltered and speak volumes. It shows a man's frustration as well as his love for his fallen firefighter son whom he spent nine months searching for at Ground Zero.

I hope that these 44 stories and memoirs in Paul Geidel's incredible book and the beautiful, artful and melodic way with which he tells them are remembered forever in the annals of history - both in New York City history and for anyone who has ever worked in the fire department or simply admired those who selflessly run into burning buildings while everyone else is running out.

- Gary Marlon Suson, New York, January 2017

BOOK ACKNOWLEDGEMENTS

1.

"I met Paul (or "Mr. Geidel" as he was introduced to me) when I was seven years old. As a single parent of two young girls, my mother was very careful about who she let into lives. Which tells you what an impression he made on her, and eventually my sister and me. For the next few years he included us in his life and the lives of his four kids - ball games, picnics, the circus, you name it. He made sure we felt loved, safe and of course always knowing the fire exits! These things may seem trivial, but to a young girl without a father in her life at the time, they were life changing. And I am blessed to still have him in my life today."

Cynthia A. Chapman, Staten Island, New York 10307

2.

To my old friend and fellow firefighter Paul,

Reading excerpts from your book brings back fond and sometimes scary memories of the experiences we shared when we were young firefighters in Rescue Co. 1. I'm now 85 years of age and I have spent half of those years (40) serving in the F.D.N.Y. Sixteen of those years were spent in rescue companies.

I have a special place in my heart and mind that I store these fond memories of the remarkable times of when we worked together. However, alongside you in that special place is a firefighter named Gary Geidel. Gary served under me when I was the company commander (Capt.) of Rescue Co.

5. Because of you, he was like family to me. He emulated you as a professional firefighter to a T. He was the epitome of what a firefighter should be. However, he came from quite an exceptional mode theft produced him. R I P Gary along

with the 342 F.D.N.Y. firefighters who perished on that fateful day,....11 of those from Rescue Co. 5.

Paul, I wish you good luck with your book and I am impressed and proud of the work you are doing with the young people out west in perpetuating the memory of that horrific tragedy of September 11, 2001. Let us ever forget!! Paul, like you I thank God every day that I was an F.D.N.Y. firefighter.

Charles J. Driscoll, Captain Rescue Co. 5 (retired)

3.

As a fellow Brother Firefighter I will be able to relate to the stories. Experience from a fellow brothers perspective life on the East Coast. Most of al,I Relate to a Fellow Brother who has seen and Experienced the *Gift of Life*, and *Living*, the *Tragic theft and of passing of Life*, and most of all the *BROTHERHOOD* to just let you know,,,,,,,

I still HAVE YOUR BACK!!!! NOW and FOR ALWAYS!

ONCE A BROTHER ALWAYS A BROTHER!!

I AM MY BROTHERS KEEPER!!!

I SHALL ALWAYS REMEMBER 09/11/2001

Randy Brown, Director

Steuben County Emergency Management

FF/Paramedic, Retired

4.

"Paul Geidel can tell real fire stories because he has lived them. There are many who'd like to believe they have gone down that long, dark smoky hallway. But Paul has, and then responded to another, even longer and darker job and prevailed. Some firefighters just tell stories, others lead the way. Let's go Paul, I'm right behind you." Paul Hashagen, Rescue 1 1983-2003. Stay safe

5.

I met Paul at the World Trade Center site. Both of us searching the debris for family members. He his son , myself my brother. We shared membership in the same unfortunate club. I looked up to Paul, all he has been thru in life and still holding strong and pushing forward. Thank you Paul for being a leader, and continuing the fight.

Rob Carlo FDNY Retired Ladder 23

6.

I met Paul right after the September 11th attacks on the World Trade Center, where he was trying to recover his son Gary. I was digging at Ground Zero attempting to find my missing Friends. I had an instant connection to Paul. We both were Firemen, Air Force Aircrew, Fishermen and Clammers. He had my back down at the site, and made sure I stayed safe as I was soon to deploy overseas and fight the War on Terror. He has so many interesting stories. Sit back and enjoy--you're about to embark on amazing adventure.

Sandy J. Krigel, Lt Col, United States Air Force (Ret)

7.

The Rescue company....a unique type of unit that is manned by highly trained and dedicated firefighters and led by hand picked officers. There are only five Rescue units in the city of New York; one in each borough. In this relatively small community of just over a 125 firefighters, everyone knows the "players", those individuals who have stood out for some reason. Paul Geidel was one of them.... his reputation was known to all in the Rescue community for his skill as a firefighter, his positive attitude and of course, his sense of humor. Paul was a leader and a friend for many years; I am happy to see he finally decided to write something other than a fire report. Good luck my friend.

John Vigiano

Rescue 2

1972 - 1973

1977 - 1988

8.

"Paul's stories are a testament to a life lived and a life loved. Paul is one of those guys you just sit and listen to for hours because he makes history come alive."

- Chris Gantz, Skokie Fire Dept. & Remembrance Rescue Project

9.

I did now know Paul when he was in the military or FDNY,

but I'm very lucky and proud to be his friend. His stories are exciting, they make me laugh or cry, but I learn a little more about what he endured as a firefighter or gunner. He is my hero and I love him very much.

Carmen Haynes, Henderson, Nevada.

10.

Fifteen years ago a man and his son walked into a tent after doing what no human being should have to do. He was searching for the remains of his son. Over the next several months I would share many meals with him during the recovery of 9/11 and slowly he would open up and start recalling stories. As the stories grew an unlikely friendship grew. Fifteen years later I am so proud to call this man who has given so much service and sacrifice to this country and the City my friend. I'm honored that I've been able to hear these stories first hand, stories that will make you gasp, cry and laugh. I think the world of you, Bobo and "thank you for your service" just doesn't seem like enough. Love you

Alisha Betten

11.

I was very blessed to have met Paul (Lt. Geidel) about out four years ago on face book and immediately knew he was my kind of guy! Not only was he a Legendary Fireman and Officer of one of the Greatest Fire Departments in the world but a genuine great man, his love for God, family and country are very prevalent in his stories and when speaking to him not to mention he has a great sense of humor. I am very happy to finally see him writing, sharing his accounts of many years of his life spent In harms way. he writes with such affliction of what it was like to be a Fireman and Boss of one of the World's Busiest & Elite Fire Rescue Companies, Paul is a Fireman's Fireman.

Lt. Tony Buckrop (Retired)

Gary, IN Fire Dept.

Squad Co. 2

12.

Like most of us, Paul's life is filled with joys and sorrows. He has dedicated his life to the service of others. From the "Frozen Chosin" of Korea to Rescue One in The New York City Fire Department, his bravery is exceptional.

On a more personal note, Paul and his lovely wife Barbara have been close friends for many, many years. This fascinating man, Paul Geidel has an extraordinary sense of humor filled with intelligence and wit. His wicked humor is dark, dark, dark. He is also an accomplished debater. No subject is off limits and there isn't much he doesn't know. I so miss a spirited repartee with Paul, especially politics and history. Did I mention he is a consummate photographer? The absolute best. This brilliant man not only lived an amazing adventure, he has taken all of us who have had the pleasure of knowing him on an amazing ride. Thank you

Lois DeStefano, Linden, New Jersey........lifelong friend

13.

"These are stories that need to be told. I have had the pleasure of Paul recounting his adventures in person, and this book has all of my favorites. He is a gifted storyteller and now I will be able to share his experiences with others, bravo!"

Steve Yeager, Jamul, CA long time friend of Paul's

14.

I have know Paul, and his family, since the mid 50's. We worked side by side in the elite Rescue Company 1, and can tell all who read his book, that he is, and did everything that the book depicts.

Captain Tom Bonamo, FDNY (ret)

15.

Paul is my **friend**, **Korean War** "Hero", 9/11/2001 Ground Zero Rescue Recovery "Hero", proud family man, fast pitch softball legend, pool shark.

His book, "Into Harms Way", with his awesome images, will make one that reads it understand why I call him "Hero".

David Joseph O'Neil, 9 months Ground Zero Rescue/Recovery worker,. Pennsylvania

1

94TH STREET FIRE

February 3, 1973

On February 3, 1976, I was the officer in command of Rescue Company 1, FDNY. Just after midnight we responded to a second alarm at East 94th Street, Manhattan.

Upon arrival, seen on the front fire escape of the building, many people were trying desperately to flee from the fire. The first floor rear apartment was fully involved with fire. We were informed by the Chief in charge that two people had already lost their lives on that floor. He ordered me to get above the fire and search for any trapped victims.

An engine company had stretched a hand line and was getting water on the fire in the rear apartment of the first floor. A second hand line was being brought into position backing up the first. Wearing Scott Air Packs, we proceeded to the second floor, in the hope of finding any trapped victims.

The six story building had apartments in both the front and rear. There was a staircase running up the middle of the building. We made a quick search of the second floor rear apartment which was just above the fire. The apartment below was engulfed in a heavy body of fire, it had extended to the rear room of the second floor.

Retreating back to the staircase closing the door behind, I called over my radio for a third hand line to knock down or hold the extending fire. In a matter of minutes an engine company had stretched their line to the front door on the second floor. Only after the engine company gotten water in their line operating, were we able to continue our search of the upper floors. They were able to knock down the fire advancing in this apartment. Visibility from the smoke and heat made this task virtually unbearable. Searching above the fire is always extremely dangerous.

We continued our search as quickly as possible, the third, fourth and fifth floor rear apartments as the engine company was holding back the fire on the second floor. The front apartments, we observed, were relatively clear of smoke and heat.

When we reached the sixth floor the heat and smoke was extensive! In my thoughts, I questioned, "why, when we left our firehouse from midtown 43rd St., hadn't the roof already been vented prior to our arrival?"

We continued our search, opening apartment doors. As fate goes, in one of the apartment rooms, lying on the floor were a number of unconscious victims. The heat and smoke had mushroomed at the top floor rendering the victims unconscious. Immediately, I called for the rest of the company to help me with getting these people out!

I grabbed a young teenage girl and carried her to a room in the front of the building which was relatively clear of smoke. The rest of the members of Rescue 1 carried and removed more of the victims to the same room. Almost immediately, assisted by a ladder company all victims were removed.

Due to the situation, all of us, began external cardiac massage along with mouth to mouth resuscitation. I was exhausted and another member from my company spelled me off with helping the teenage girl.

Once I had a minute to back off, and observe, I looked about the apartment room and saw a team of firefighters working to save every one of these victims. Their extensive training was now being put to the task. I was so very proud of all of them. Unfortunately, we failed! We were not able to save anyone. They all succumbed from smoke inhalation. It will remain a sight during my lifetime that I will never forget!!

Looking back to this day, I can't understand why some of these people didn't try to make their way to the front fire escape. The rear was virtually impossible due to the fire escape being totally engulfed in flames.

In newspaper clipping below, Firefighter Flip Mullen of Rescue 1 is pictured helping an elderly woman to safety.

OVER THE COUNTER

FIRE KILLS 10

7 Children Are Victims In West Side Tenement

By William T. Slattery
and Richard Schwartz

Hunt 3 in Priest Killing

By Robert Garrett
and Cy Egan

2

OFF TO KOREA BROKEN

1952

It was off to Langley Air Force Base (AFB) after graduating B-26 Invader gunnery school at Lowery AFB, Denver Co.. The time period was around Aug.-Sept. 1952. At Langley I was assigned the gunner of a combat crew on the Douglas Invader B-26. Three men made up a combat crew, a pilot, navigator/bombardier and gunner. We trained as a crew at Langley in air to ground combat techniques, which included strafing, bombing and gunnery.

My gunnery training included shooting bullets from an altitude of 500 foot into the ocean below. This training mission was called a "Splash" mission. I would fire short bursts of 50 calibers, causing a splash in the water. The splash then became the target. It was my job to hit the target with a second short burst. With the B-26 traveling at over 200 mph, I had to allow for Kentucky Windage. I hit the target every time.

Kentucky Windage, a slang word is a method of correcting for wind, gravity, air speed, etc., by aiming a weapon to one side of a target instead of by adjusting the sights.

In Korea we used Armor Piercing Incendiary 50 caliber. (API) The API's exploded on impact causing a bright flash. You could adjust, again using Kentucky Windage hitting the target.

Back at Langley. After finishing combat crew training we were given a 30 day leave before heading out to Korea.

While on leave I had good times with my family and friends. At one point, while with my buddies I was riding on the hood of a car. The driver thinking it was funny accelerated, then slammed on the brakes causing me to be thrown to the ground. I landed on my wrist. My wrist swelled, but not enough for me to see a doctor. I didn't want to screw up my shipping out to Korea.

There was one more school to attend before shipping overseas to Korea. It was a 15 day/night survival trading course at Stead AFB, located just 12 miles north of Reno, Nevada. This course was designed to instruct us how to survive over land if ever forced down in enemy territory. We learned how to fish, make rock ovens, meat jerky, use our parachute lanyards to make fish nets and fish lines, etc. Our survival kit contained a map of the area, fish hooks, a knife, matches and a warm sleeping bag. "Jerky" is long strips of meat that are preserved by smoking over an open fire.

After the first six days of concentrated practical training on the base, the crews were moved to a nearby mountain wilderness to undergo a survival trek, made as realistic as possible. Under conditions of extreme stress, your capacity, or incapacity, to survive is tested.

Navigators, gunners, pilots--------you all learn that anything covered with fur or feathers is edible and all eggs are nourishing until hatched.

Our crew passed with flying colors and it was off to Korea.

My orders assigned me to the 17th Bomb Wing, 95th Bomb Squadron, K-9 AFB, in Pusan, Korea. This outfit was the famed Doolittle Raiders Bomb Group that bombed Tokyo, Japan on April 18, 1942.

I arrived in Korea Nov. 3, 1952, the start of a long cold winter. After flying 43 combat missions over North Korea, ending my combat tour, I was assigned the job as Duty Gunner. The Duty Gunner was to take combat crews to and from their aircraft during all hours at night.

I wanted to get out of this assignment in the worst way. I decided to go to the flight surgeon and have my wrist checked due to pain. X-rays were taken which showed a break in the neck of the Nonvascular. I flew all 43 combat missions with a broken wrist and never knew it!!!

Leaving Korea I was assigned to the 509th Bomb Wing, 393rd Bomb Squadron, at Roswell AFB, Roswell, New Mexico. The 393rd Bomb Squadron was the famed Col. Paul Tibbitts squadron that dropped the atomic bomb "Little Boy" Aug 6th, 1945 on Hiroshima, Japan.

The flight surgeon placed my arm in a cast for two months. The cast was removed and the bone healed perfectly.

Pictured of the cast placed on my right wrist at Roswell, AFB, New Mexico.

I was extremely proud to be assigned to two historical bomber squadrons in my four year enlistment.

3

CHRISTMAS RESCUE

1975

December 23, 1975, I was the officer in charge working a night tour (6 PM to AM) at Rescue Company 1, FDNY in mid-town Manhattan, New York. It was early into our tour and we were just getting ready to sit down and enjoy rib eye steaks off the barbeque. Everyone was hungry. The dinner table was set with a hot baked potato on each plate, when an alarm came in. Another meal ruined at the sound of the bell!

As we were responding to the fire, the department radio call gave us the street address. Once we arrived, we noticed fire companies up to a block away were already at the scene.

However, before we arrived at that address, we were waved down by frantic people on the street. They pointed to a fire in the five story tenement building next to us. Wow! Two fires on the same street, at the same time!! We pulled over to the curb. I radioed the new address to the Battalion Chief in charge.

Fire was visible from the front and side windows of the top floor. Wearing our Scott Air Packs,

Firefighter James Curran also from Rescue Company 1, and I went down an alley, alongside the building to the rear. Hearing cries for help, I looked up and saw two heads sticking out of a top floor side window. Heavy black smoke was seen bellowing out around their heads.

We were on the move. However, an anchor fence, which was about twenty feet from the building, prevented us from getting to the rear fire escape. We took off our Scotts making it easier for us to climb over the fence. Damn, the fire escape drop ladder was still in place but out of our reach. Luckily, Curran was carrying a six foot hook and was able to push the drop ladder up so as to release it, bringing it to the ground.

Curran was the first to climb the ladder as I followed. Once we got to the top floor, Curran continued to the roof. I broke through a rear bedroom window from the fire escape and climbed on to the fire floor. Since smoke and heat was pushing out over my head, I got as low to the floor as possible. I crawled across the room, down a hallway towards the people I heard screaming for help!

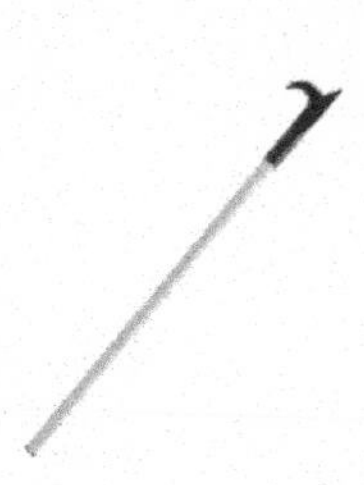

Fire was rolling across the hallway ceiling over my head. I crawled over a very large, unconscious dog lying on the hallway floor. Continuing down the hallway I reached the room where I heard the calls for help. As I continued my search, staying low, I noticed two naked men by the window. I crawled inside and immediately grabbed one man by his arm, pulling him back to the doorway, yelling for the other to follow. The fire was extending from the hallway ceiling, through the transom above, and into the room.

I pushed the one man ahead of me. We crawled safely back down the hallway, to the fire escape. Yes, I could clearly see his naked ass!!!! I looked back and noticed that the second man was not following!

During my search and rescue, three firefighters from Ladder Company 35 had entered the rear bedroom from the fire escape. They proceeded to breach the wall to the room where the victims were trapped.

I crawled back down the hallway for a second time hoping to rescue the other man. I entered the room and made a quick search through the heat and smoke. Fire continued burning above along the ceiling.

However, he was gone! I figured he may have jumped out the window.

Suddenly, I felt a hand reach out to me from the breached wall. It was a member of Ladder Company 35. I climbed through the hole they made. We all

Firefighter in daring rescue of 2

A Tottenville fire lieutenant pulled two men from a burning apartment in Midtown Manhattan yesterday after climbing up five stories on a fire escape.

Fire officials said the fire at 530 West 43rd St., was coming out of two windows when firemen from Rescue Co. One arrived and spotted two men screaming for help from a fifth floot window.

Lt. Paul Geidel went up a fire escape to the apartment and broke through a bedroom window. In order to get to the trapped men, Geidel had to crawl through a room, where he grabbed onto the men, Mignel Vargas and Esto Martinez, both about 35, and escorted them back to the fire escape.

Geidel and the men were treated for smoke inhalation and burns, officials reported.

According to fire officials, Geidel was recommended for a Fire Department citation.

bailed out of the floor onto the safety of the fire escape.

Unknown to me at the time, Ladder Company 35 had pulled the other man out of the apartment through the breached wall.

The victim's who both were about thirty five years old were Mignel Vargas and Esto Martinez. We all were treated for burns and smoke inhalation at the scene. Sadly, I never found out if the dog survived.

The reporter who wrote this article made a few mistakes. The address used in this article is the headquarters of Rescue Company 1 and not the fire address as written.

Also, I rescued only one of the men not two.

4

FALLEN BRICKS

1970

It was a beautiful summer night in Brooklyn. I was the covering officer for Lieutenant Richard Hamilton, Rescue Company 2, F.D.N.Y., who was on vacation.

After roll call, I gave each member his assignment for our tour. Jobs consisted of roof man, outside vent, can man, (2 ½ gal water fire extinguisher), and the forcible entry team. Then we had a drill on cutting metal with an oxygen-acetylene torch.

Once done, we headed for the dinner table.

During the meal an alarm was transmitted for a fire in the Brownsville section of Brooklyn. We would only respond if the fire got out of control.

Immediately, a 10-75, a signal for a working fire, was transmitted for this box! We suited up. I gave the order to start going to the fire, even before we were called. On the way over, the all hands were transmitted for which we were assigned. (An all hands is when all company's at the fire are put to work) We had a head start to the location and arrived quickly.

Once off our rig we headed to our assigned jobs. Roof man to the roof, the outside vent man to his job, etc., and the others, including myself to the fire floor.

Once we reached the fire floor we saw that the ladder company was pulling ceilings. The engine company was operating a hand line. Most of the visible fire was being knocked down.

While searching a bedroom, we found lying on a bed an unconscious male civilian. Firefighter Artie Conley, R-2, immediately gave him mouth-to-mouth resuscitation and external cardiac message.

I radioed to the R-2 chauffer to bring the resuscitator to the fire floor. While the fire was being fought we continued to aid the victim while he was lying on the bed. Once the resuscitator arrived, we gave him oxygen.

Meantime, another member of R-2 brought up the Stokes, a wire stretcher formed to shape a victim, so we could get the victim to the hospital as quickly as possible. After placing the victim in the Stokes, we proceeded to transport him out of the building. However, tragedy struck!!

A huge cluster of about ten or more cemented house bricks came crashing through the skylight above the staircase. They landed directly on the chest of the victim!!

The weight of the bricks was a crushing blow to the victim and almost caused us to drop the Stokes. I had no idea what injuries he sustained. We quickly got him to the street below, into a waiting ambulance.

Later, we learned that the victim did not make it, he died. We had no idea if it was from the smoke or the bricks landing on his chest.

Whenever there is a loss of life at a fire, an investigation follows. So, it was no surprise that I was personally called by the Deputy Chief in charge asking me questions of our involvement.

The Deputy Chief interrogated me. He questioned...

- How were we able to get to the fire scene so quickly?
- Why we gave the victim mouth-to-mouth and external cardiac massage?

- How did I know he was unconscious?
- How did I know he wasn't in cardiac fibrillation?

His questions leaned toward the possibility that we were responsible for the death of this man. I wasn't going to allow this!!

I fired right back and told him we followed the proper protocol which is spelled out in the all units circular *(a manual printed by FDNY on job procedures)*. The manual clearly states that mouth-to-mouth and external cardiac massage is to be given immediately, not wasting precious seconds checking for a pulse or breathing.

I also told the chief that a huge cluster of bricks came crashing down on the victims chest. He huffed, puffed and grumbled as he told me I was excused and to get out of his office!

To this day, I can't understand why that cluster of bricks came crashing through the skylight. The timing was bad.

Who did it? Why? Questions I never asked?

5

NURSE

January 30, 1962

It was a cold winter morning around 5 AM when a fire alarm was transmitted to Rescue Company 1, located on 43rd Street between 5th and 6th Avenues.

The fire was reported on the fourth floor of a thirteen-story building at 10 Mitchell Place, Manhattan.

The first due engine company arrived and hooked up their hose line to the third floor stand-pipe, and then stretched it to the fourth floor. (See stand-pipe).

After getting water in their line, they knocked down all visible fire in the fire apartment. Rescue Company 1 was ordered to make a complete search of

the fire floor and floors above the fire. Once there, I crawled down a hallway, staying as low as possible to the floor, below the heat and smoke level. I searched the one room apartment and came upon an unconscious female lying on the floor. With the assistance of rescue members we removed the victim immediately to the floor below the fire.

Sadly, I am shown on the front page of the New York Mirror newspaper trying in vain to revive Mrs. Eva Allen, 75, as priest Father John O'Reilly gives last rites. It was later learned that she lived alone. It was another sad day working with Rescue Company 1.

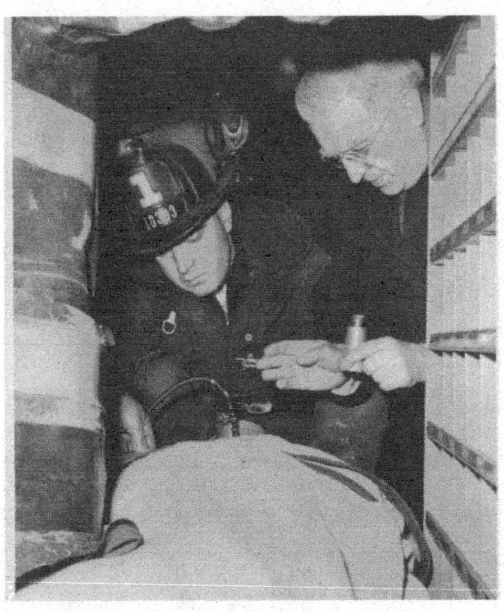

6

BOMBER STREAM OVER NORTH KOREA

January 15, 1953

Korea, January 15th 1953, K-9 AFB, Pusan, at 0230 hours nine Douglas B-26 Invaders are warming up engines, They are getting ready for a Bomber Stream combat mission over North Korea. After a one hour pre-briefing of all combat crews, the Pathfinder (lead aircraft) of the Stream prepared for takeoff at 0230, followed 30 minutes later at 5 minute intervals, (0300, 0305 hours) the remaining eight aircraft.

The lead aircraft, the Pathfinder is carrying a bomb load of incendiary bombs to start as many fires as possible at the target so the incoming aircraft can see where to drop there ordinance.

Each of the remaining eight B-26's is carrying a bomb load of ten 500 pound bombs, two under each wing, and six in the bomb bay.

All aircraft is flying north, at an altitude of 2000 feet above mountainous terrain, following one another five minutes apart.

The Pathfinders responsibility was to locate the pre-briefed target, bomb and start fires, climb to an altitude of 3000 feet, orbit the target and direct each of the incoming aircraft as to where to drop their bomb load in relation to the fires started on the ground. After the last of the eight aircraft left the target area, Pathfinder's was to take photographs showing the results of the mission. The Pathfinder's time over the target is approximately one hour and fifteen minutes. The rest of the Stream, one run, had only a few minutes over the target.

At this point, it was extremely scary and death defying. If the target had heavy triple A (anti-aircraft artillery) protection, the Pathfinder would be exposed to it from both the two thousand foot altitude and the three thousand foot altitude. If there were search lights, your chances were even worse getting through.

My B-26 was the fifth aircraft on the Stream following the Pathfinder. We were twenty minutes behind the number two aircraft. The night was dark, but clear, and as we got closer to the target, both automatic and heavy triple A could be seen coming up at the number two aircraft. It could be seen clearly this far out. It reminded me, back home, of the Roman Candles during Fourth of July, only hundreds of them at the same time.

Getting hosed was a term used when so much flak came at you at once. Then the quiet between the five minute intervals between each aircraft. Occasionally a few triple A's firing at the Pathfinder was visible. As the target got closer, flak was seen more clearly, the aircraft ahead getting hosed. Once again, the five minute quiet.

When we were five minutes out, the flak coming up at the aircraft in front of us was one of the most fearful moments of my life! I was praying they made it though. Again, the five minute quiet before our run over the target. When we reached the target I can honestly say it was over. We were lit up by search lights and the hosing was intense. We were directed by Pathfinder where to drop our bombs, we dropped them, and flew right through it all unscathed. I was amazed, asking myself how the hell are we making it though all this flak? It was coming up at us from every direction, left, right, ahead and even down from the mountain tops.

However, all B-26's returned safely to K-9, and an inspection of all aircraft revealed that there were only a few minor holes in the wing and the tail of three of the aircraft. Photographs that were taken by the Pathfinder after the last aircraft finished its bomb run showed the target was 100% covered and destroyed.

The following month, I was on my second Bomber Stream combat mission. I was the gunner on the Pathfinder aircraft of Colonel Delwin Bentley, the squadron commander of the 95th Bomb Squadron. I flew next to him in the co-pilots seat. But, that's "Another Story."

At this point I had about fifteen combat missions completed with thirty five to go. Oh boy!!

7

ANOTHER STORY

March 5, 1953

The moon was full. I was preparing for another Bomber Stream night mission. It was 0200 in the morning and extremely cold. I was the gunner assigned to fly with pilot Colonel Delwin Bentley. Colonel Bentley was the squadron commander of 95th Bomb Squadron, 17th Bomb Group. It was my 30th combat mission. We were the Pathfinder aircraft followed by eight other B-26's. Our takeoff time was at 0300 followed at 0330 the first of the eight B-26's in the Stream each taking off at 5 minute intervals.

Colonel Bentley was from Casper, Wyo. A World War II seasoned combat veteran who flew the B-26 Martin Marauders over France and Germany. He was a highly skilled fearless pilot, a warrior and risk taker. He piloted the Douglas B-26 like no other, and treated as if it were a fighter not an attack bomber.

The Colonel had me ride the right seat not the gunner's compartment. He wanted me to be another set of eyes looking out from the cockpit for automatic and heavy triple AAA ground fire fired at us, also to take notes on each bomb drop, the heading and results.

Our target was a small town named Samho just north of Hungnam Harbor in east North Korea. We flew directly over the Chosen Reservoir. During the battle at the Chosen Reservoir, the Marines surrounded, fought their way out to Hungnam Harbor. Looking down at those snow covered mountains I fully realized how cold it was during that battle and what our troops went through. It was 20 degrees below zero while flying at our altitude. What I read about that battle, it was called the Frozen Chosen. It was colder during the battle of the Chosen Reservoir, then in our aircraft, and cold it was.

Our altitude was 2000ft above the terrain. Once our target was located the Colonel did something different. Instead of staying at 2000ft he dropped down to about 500ft for a closer look. Two search lights immediately lit up the sky searching for us. Before the lights locked in on us, the Colonel quickly turned our B-26 making a strafing run directly at the lights. He fired six 50 caliber wing mounted machine guns knocking out both search lights in one short burst

Our ordinance was incendiary bombs carried under each wing and fully loaded in the bomb bay. The incendiary bombs were filled with combustible chemicals such as magnesium, phosphorus or petroleum jelly napalm. They were dropped in clusters to spread fires. They were eighteen inches long and weighted only a couple pounds. They were dropped in containers of different sizes. The average "cluster" was seventy-two incendiaries.

The Colonel made two low level bomb runs dropping wing mounted bombs, immediately setting structures on fire. Then climbing back to the 2000ft altitude.

During this time we were encountering inaccurate ground fire. The ground fire was from automatic weapons and looked like flaming golf balls (Roman Candles). This was coming up at us from all directions.

Back at 2000ft we continued dropping the remainder of our bombs setting as many buildings on fire as possible. The target must have been a munitions storage facility because of the many secondary explosions. I made recordings of roofs being blown into the air and the many buildings set on fire. Each building hit was immediately involved in fire. I lost count of the explosions and buildings afire. It was a sight to remember.

After our thirty minute time period over the target area we climbed to an altitude of 3000ft. As each of the B-26's in the Stream arrived the Colonel instructed them where to drop their ordinance, to the left or the right of certain buildings on fire. As each B-26 made its bomb run they received automatic ground fire from every direction. I witnessed each B-26 in the Stream make its bomb drop successfully not getting hit.

We remained over the target until the last B-26 made its bomb drop. We took photographs of the target area for results and headed back home. Our time over the target area was about one hour and twenty minutes. The other aircraft in the stream was over target no more than two minutes. All during this time period we encountered frequent ground fire without let up. I thanked God for their inaccuracy.

After returning to K-9 AFB we went to the debriefing building. The Colonel made his report. Photos of the mission showed the target was 100% destroyed.

Shortly after the mission I was in the 95th Bomb Squadron Quonset hut headquarters when a clerk showed me the citation recommending me for the Distinguished Flying Cross, (DFC) for the Samho mission.

This paper work signed by Colonel Bentley, was then forwarded to 5th Air Force headquarters for approval. While flying my remaining combat missions, finishing at forty three, I was informed that many of the crew members on the Stream received the DFC for their participation in the Samho mission.

Two weeks after flying my last combat mission I was transferred to Walker AFB, Roswell, New Mexico. About one year later I received paper work awarding me two Air Medals for my forty three combat missions over North Korea and the Presidential Unit Citation. To this day the DFC remains a mystery.

8

ANKLE MAN

December 8, 1968

At ten o'clock on a Sunday morning, Rescue Company 1 got a call to respond to 42nd St. and Park Avenue, Manhattan, N.Y.C. When we arrived at the scene we noticed a crowd of people looking upward. High above at the 15th floor of this building there was a man dangling from a window with what appeared to be a rope or strap.

What the hell is this all about?

We grabbed our first aid gear and headed towards the building. I was the first one to enter the elevator, but in no time it was packed tightly with firefighters and I was pushed to the rear corner.

When we got to the 15th floor, the elevator doors opened and we all ran down the hallway in the same direction. I was last in line because I was crushed in the back of the elevator. However, we soon realized that we were going in the wrong direction. We did an about face and I was now leading the pack.

Looking in an open doorway, I saw an elderly man on top of a fourteen inch window sill holding a hand. It was the hand of a window washer, his back was to the building, helplessly dangling from only one of his safety straps and he slipped from the window sill.

I told the elderly man to get out of the way as I climbed on the window sill and took off my boots.

Firefighter (FF) Bill "Moose" Curran handed me a roof rope. Then he and FF Henry Kroger, both from Rescue Company 1, lowered me by my ankles out the window.......to a point of no return.

Dangling next to the window washer I said, "We have to stop meeting like this."

I looked down the fifteen stories and the people down there appeared to be small ants. Needless, to say, I was really scared.

"What is your name?" I asked. He responded weakly, "Andy." "Andy, try not to move while I tie this rope around your body under your arm pits."

After I got through tying the rope around him I was pulled back up into the safety of the building.

Now the three of us pulled Andy, who weighed at least 220 pounds, back up through the window using the rope I tied around his body. No easy task.

While pulling Andy to safety, I prayed the knot I tied around him would not fail. If it did, living that memory would remain with me forever.

Thankfully, we managed to get a shaken Andy back into the building!!! I may not have had any stains in my pants, but I can't speak for Andy!

From the street below we heard a loud cheering coming from the crowd. I could only imagine the apprehension they were going through during this rescue.

For quite a while my new name at Rescue 1 was "Ankle Man!" The Staten Island Advance, a local newspaper followed up title.

Islander Ankle-Man In 15th-Floor Rescue

A Tottenville fireman was lowered head-first from a 15th-floor window of a Manhattan office building Saturday to rescue a 220-pound window cleaner suspended dizzily from only one safety hook.

Paul Geidel, 29, of 378 Sleight Ave., a member of Fire Rescue 1, scrambled out the ledge of Pershing Square Building at E. 42nd St. and Park Ave. to reach the frantic man, Andrew M. Bey, 58, of Newark, N.J.

Geidel went out the ledge head first, with other firemen holding his ankles, and slipped one rope under Bey's shoulders and another around his life belt

"The thing was the time element," Geidel said. "There was no telling when the other strap might break. He could have slipped through the safety harness at any time."

* * *

BEY said he lost his balance after fastening one of his two safety hooks and toppled below the window, dangling by the secured hook with his back to the wall.

An elevator operator in the building, informed of Bey's plight, reached the scene and, with the aid of others, maintained a grip on Bey until firemen were able to haul him up.

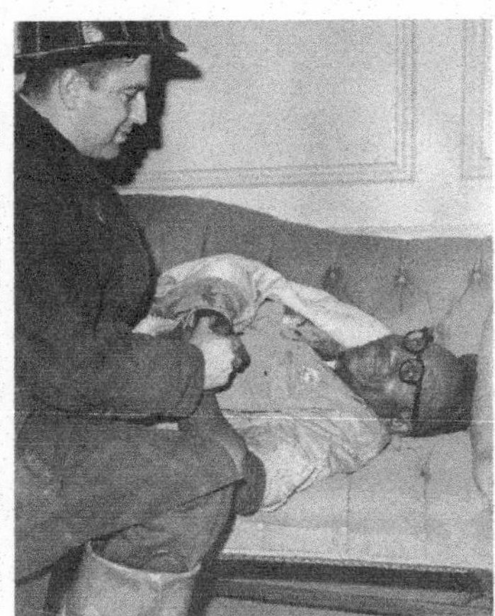

Clutches Sill 15 Floors Up, Then, Whew!

By WILLIAM NEUGEBAUER

For 15 agonizing minutes yesterday a 6-foot-2, 220-pound window cleaner dangled from a sill of a midtown building, only his clutching fingers and one safety hook holding him from death on the sidewalk 15 stories below.

Then an elevator operator in the building, the Pershing Square Building, E. 42d St. and Park Ave., lent his meager support—he's 5-foot-7, 150 pounds. He grasped the wrists of the window cleaner, Andrew M. Bey, 59, father of three, of 32 Chester Ave., Newark.

But it took firemen from several companies to loop a line around Bey's waist and draw the heavy man to safety. First they threw out a safety net at the 11th floor.

The dramatic rescue began at 9:40 A.M. when the elevator operator, Edward Kearns, 62, of

(NEWS foto by Frank Castoral)
Fireman Paul Geidel tells of pulling Andrew Bey to safety.

103-54 93d St., Ozone Park, Queens, grandfather of three, was finishing a coffee break.

Passerby Screams

"Hey, there's a man dangling from the window sill by his fingers," screamed a passerby who had rushed into the lobby.

Kearns looked outside for a cop. Finding none, he rushed with the unidentified passerby and a mailman up to the 15th floor. Kearns knew it would be Bey, an acquaintance of 20 years. Minutes before, he had left Bey at that level.

by held him. Kearns leaned out below the window sill and grasped Bey's hands. Finally, two engine companies, two truck companies and a fire rescue company arrived below.

Goes Out Head First

Deputy Chief Bernard Dolberger of the 3d Division ordered the net thrown up under Bey, who hung from a window of the William Esty Co. advertising agency on the Park Ave. side.

Fireman Paul Geidel, 29, of 378 Sleigh Ave., Tottenville, S.I., attached to Fire Rescue 1, went out the window head first while others held his ankles and attached a rope to Bey's waist.

Pulled to safety, he was rushed to Grand Central Hospital for treatment for shock.

Loses Balance

Bey said he had fastened his left safety buckle to a hook and was trying to attach the right when he lost his balance and toppled below the window.

His back to the wall, he gripped the ledge and screamed for help.

JFK & Party At Army-Navy

Philadelphia, Dec. 1 (Special)—President Kennedy took British Ambassador David Ormsby-Gore and his wife to the Army-Navy game here today in a small party of old personal friends.

The group came from Washington by helicopter and returned by train.

Kennedy, the old PT-boat skipper, sat on Navy's side of the field in the first half, then switched to Army's.

On his return to the capital, the President took a helicopter to Glen Ora, Va., to join his family for a quite weekend. Jackie, who prefers a good fox hunt to a football game, was already there.

9

RACHEL

1974

It was a rainy, wet, summer night on or about two in the morning when we returned to Rescue Company 1, FDNY after a fire.

The firehouse was located between 9th and 10th Ave, on 43rd St, Manhattan, NYC. The overhead door was open for girl watching.

It was late for girl watching, but we still waited. Because it is Manhattan you never knew who might pass by the firehouse. While standing inside the doorway we heard the sound of a woman's heel hitting the wet sidewalk. Just the sound of one heel, not two.

I walked out to the sidewalk to see a woman in a short, short skirt, low cut blouse, knee high boots, chewing gum, swinging her butt. Her purse, which she held in one hand, moving back and forth. In the other hand she carried the heel of a shoe. It had just stopped raining, but saw she did not have an umbrella.

She walked up to me and said, "Misster fi-er mans, can you fix ma shoe?"

I respond "sure, what's your name."

"Ma name is Rachel."

Then I called to one of the firemen, "Jessie, help this young lady out and fix the heel on her shoe."

"It is dangerous to be out here this late at night. What are you doing up this late?" I asked.

Looking at me like I was so, so dumb, naïve, she said, "It's ma job, this is what I do, this what I do, it's ma job."

Of course I knew what she did. However, I acted like a light bulb just went off in my head, and said "Oh my, that is such a dangerous job.""Jessie, hurry up with that shoe," I yelled. "Rachel, what does one pay for your services?"

After a long, long delay, she looked at me and answered, "truck drivers $40-$45 dallars...(delay).....Bus drivers $40 dallars... (delay)....Regulars $30 dallars... ....(another long, long, long delay).....fi-er mans FAVE."

At this point, I ignored giving her any kind of response.

Jessie gave her the repaired shoe as we thanked her for the information. We wished her well as we escorted her out the door listening to the sound of two heels, rather than one, hitting the sidewalk walking away into the night.

This was life in mid-town Manhattan before Mayor Giuliani started to clean up.

10

COMBAT CREW

1952

After gunnery school in June of 1952 at Lowry Air Force Base in Denver, CO it was off to combat crew training at Langley AFB in Virginia for combat crew training on the Douglas B-26 Invader.

During our crew training there, we learned skip bombing, strafing, bombing and gunnery splash missions. A splash mission was when we flew about 400 feet above the ocean, I was to shoot a burst of 50 cal. bullets into the ocean. When the bullets hit the water I was to fire another burst of 50's and hit the splash of the previous firing. I found it pretty easy to hit the splash even though we were flying at a high rate of speed and you still needed Kentucky Wind age to hit your target. (Kentucky Wind age, an adjustment made by a shooter to correct for wind (or motion of the target) by aiming at a point horizontal to the target's position in the sight rather than by adjusting the sight to compensate.)

After two months of extensive crew training we were assigned a combat crew. We were given a three week leave and then off to Stead AFB for a three week survival crew training in route to Korea.

After arriving at K-1 AFB, West Pusan, South Korea, it was a few more combat training missions, (bombing, strafing, and gunnery) before flying our first of 55 combat missions.

I was assigned to the 17th Bomb Wing, 95th Bomb Squadron.

Early on into my combat tour, my pilot, Lt. Tate had gotten ulcers and was sent back home. That left me the gunner, and the navigator/bombardier as bastard crewman, without a pilot and a broken combat crew. We had to fly the rest of our combat tour with different crews until we reached our 55 missions.

During the following months the 55 mission requirement was dropped to 50.

In February 1953 I was the assigned the gunner to a combat crew with the pilot named Captain George Vioux and the navigator/bombardier, Captain Tom Cameron. I was to fly my remaining combat missions with this crew.

The requirement for a gunner's combat tour was dropped from 50 to 35 combat missions. I was in the middle when the order came down changing the mission requirement and flew my last, the 43rd mission with Vioux and Cameron. Pictured L/R Captain Vioux, Captain Cameron and myself A/1st Class Paul E. Geidel. This photo was taken after our last combat mission over North Korea. The second photo is my brother Richard shaking my hand that night.

Sometime in the evening during March 1953 our crew was assigned a moonlit rail reconnaissance mission. We were sent up to destroy locomotive and rail cars bringing supply's to the front line troops. Our assignment was north of Wonsan Harbor, and around the Chosen Reservoir area on the east side of the Korean peninsula. It was our last combat mission together, we were finally going home.

It was a moonlit night and cursing about 500 feet altitude we were following the reflection of the moon off the railroad tracks leading north. Occasionally we received some AAA automatic weapon fire but the rounds were not even close. There was no need to make any evasive action.

Continuing north the navigator/bombardier spotted a convoy of trucks going south along on a mountain road with their headlights on. It was our last mission so the pilot elected to take out as many trucks as possible. If we spotted a train that would have been our primary target. The pilot lined up for a bomb drop on the lead truck. We dropped two 500 lbs. cutting the road in half just in front of the convoy. The trucks now were backed up unable to move forward due to the massive holes in the road. Our second run we dropped another two bombs directly on the lead truck bringing it into flames. We continued making bomb drops from a safe altitude destroying as many trucks as possible. As soon as we dropped our last 500 lb. bomb the pilot resumed with strafing runs. There were three 50 cal. guns mounted in each wing. As we peeled off each strafing run I would fire from both my upper and lower turrets, API's (armor piercing incendiary) rounds (setting fire to as many trucks available. The pilot then would line up for a final strafing run using up all remaining ordinances. All suppy trucks were fully involved in fire.

We returned safely to K-9 AFB. A United States Air Force photographer was there to congratulate us and take photographs. A bottle of champagne was also on hand to celebrate our successful final mission.

11

46TH STREET FIRE

1964

It was a cool afternoon on February 22, 1964 when I was working at Rescue Co. 1 in midtown Manhattan as a member of the forcible entry team assigned to carry an ax.

An alarm was transmitted from the 46th St. location.

Rescue Company 1, as well as other companies, immediately responded. Because of the volume of fire, a second alarm immediately was transmitted by the first arriving company.

A fire had erupted on the fourth floor of a fourteen story glass/aluminum office building at 20 East 46th Street.

When we arrived, fire was blowing out all the windows on the fourth floor. Wearing a Scott Air Pak, I followed my officer into the building, up a staircase to the floor above the fire. I then began my search of the floor, looking for anyone trapped or any extension of the fire. Conditions were extremely hot with dense, black smoke!

During my search I came upon a maintenance man cowering next to an open elevator door.

"Stay low and follow me back to the staircase," I said.

However, he refused. So, I grabbed onto his arm and tried to pull him back to the staircase. He fought me! He just wanted to go into the elevator. Rather than continue the struggle with him, I foolishly went into the elevator to take him out of harm's way.

Because he didn't have a mask, I shared air with him from my Scott Air Pack. The elevator started downward, then stalled on the fire floor! All the electrical power was burnt out. I almost shit my pants!!! I knew that we were in a life threatening situation; trapped in an elevator at the fire floor. My adrenalin had reached its peak. I was scared and pissed because I knew it was basic knowledge that one should always take the staircase out of a burning building.

Then I heard screams for help coming from an adjoining elevator. I took my ax and pried open the doors of my elevator as the dense smoke poured in. I could see flames burning across the ceiling above!

"Keep low, hold on to my turnout coat, and follow me," I ordered to the maintenance man.

I knew where the staircase was and that it would lead us to safety. Because of my experience, the floor plans of these buildings were all the same. As we were crawling past the adjoining elevator, I could hear the people inside crying for help. We were only a short distance to the staircase.

In the meantime, an engine company was operating a hand line from the staircase doorway, getting water on the fire. Another group of firefighters were huddled on the staircase. As soon as we reached the staircase, I handed the maintenance man to them.

Then, I did a quick return back to the elevator where the cries of help were coming from. With the aid of firefighter Robert Post of Ladder Company 4, we were able to force open the elevator door.

Lying on the floor, was an unconscious woman. Also were five men on their knees gasping desperately for air.

The fire above continued to be knocked down by the hand line operating from the staircase. However, a ladder pipe was pouring from the outside was making conditions worse inside!!!

Firefighter Post grabbed the woman and carried her back to the staircase as he continued to the street. I dragged two of the five men out of the elevator to the safety of the staircase, yelling for the others to follow.

All the victims were treated at the scene for smoke inhalation. The woman had to be transferred to a local hospital for evaluation. She was later released.

In hindsight, entering the elevator was a colossal mistake. However, in retrospect, it turned out to be a blessing in disguise. If it were not for my elevator stalling on the fire floor, I would never have heard the other victims calling for help.

2/22/64

2 Island Firefighters Save 6 from Flames

Six persons owe their lives today to two Staten Island firemen who braved intense heat and smoke Saturday to rescue them from an elevator in which they were trapped in a burning building in Manhattan.

The firemen, Paul Geidel Jr., 30, of 378 Sleight Ave., Tottenville, and Robert Post, 31, of 244 Prescott Ave., Grant City, forced open the elevator and helped three of the people to safety. The other three made it under their own power.

The fire broke out just before noon on the fourth floor of a 14-story office building at 20 E. 46th St.

Geidel, of Rescue Co. No 1, and Post, who is with Ladder Co. No. 4, were sent to search the floor above the fire for anyone who might be trapped.

* * *

GEIDEL found a maintenance employe groping his way through the smoke and heat. They got on an elevator and started down, but the elevator stuck on the fourth floor. Geidel heard people trapped in an elevator right next to them.

Geidel broke open his elevator, helped the employe to a fire escape and returned. Meanwhile, Post, whose filter-type mask had lost its effectiveness in the intense heat, was on his way downstairs.

He and Geidel forced open the elevator and found a woman, Laura Authernac, unconscious. Post carried her down four flights to the street.

Two of the men were semiconscious. Geidel dragged them down the stairs, one under each arm. The other three men followed.

* * *

THE SIX had been trapped in the elevator for about five minutes with smoke seeping in through the doors.

Hundreds of people had gathered on the street when Geidel and Post carried the woman and two men to safety. Meanwhile, about 50 other firemen poured water onto the blaze and confined the flames to the fourth floor.

Smoker's Fire Kills B'klynite

By WILLIAM NEUGEBAUER and JOSEPH McNAMARA

A two-alarm fire, believed started by a couch smoker, quickly spread through a four-story tenement in the Bedford-Stuyvesant section of Brooklyn early yesterday and took the life of a 58-year-old man.

(NEWS foto by Arthur B

Samuel Weiss, 58, one of six trapped in elevator, is assist scene of blaze at 20 E. 46th St. by fireman.

At two other fires, six persons trapped in an elevator were saved by firemen in a midtown office building, and an elderly woman was rescued in Harlem.

50 Tenants Flee

The fatal blaze, which erupted in a second-floor flat at 88 Clifton Place at 4:05 A. M., ignited an adjacent four-story brick building at No. 86. A second alarm was turned in 10 minutes later as some 50 tenants fled to the street.

After the blaze was under control at 5 A. M., firemen found the body of McKinley Mills, a boarder, in the apartment where the fire began.

An elevator that stalled during a fire in the 14-floor office building at 20 E. 46th St., at Madison Ave., almost proved a tomb for six passengers.

But two Staten Island firemen, Paul Geidel, 30, of Rescue Co. 1, and Robert Post, 31, of Ladder 4, chopped open the doors of the elevator, which was stalled at the fourth floor.

Carried Down Stairs

All six were lying on the floor dazed and frightened. One, Laura Authenac, 27, of 111 W. 46th St., was unconscious.

Post carried the unconscious woman down the stairs to the street, while Geidel dragged two men and guided the other three.

Geidel was himself trapped in another elevator at the fifth floor, along with maintenance man Willie Cokrell, 31, who had discovered the fire. The fireman hacked his way out, raced down the stairs to the burning fourth floor to help Post rescue the six.

In the Harlem fire, at 210 W. 153d St., Battalion Chief Philip Fogler, 51, raced into a blazing smoked-clogged flat and carried badly-burned Viola Taylor, 72, to safety.

A visitor, Geroge Scott, 55, of 211 W. 153d St., was overcome by smoke. Both were taken to Harlem Hospital. Her condition is serious, his good. The fire was put out at 9 A.M.

(Other pictures on page 1)

14-L 8*R New York Journal-American, Sun., Feb. 23, 1964

Save 7 Caught in Fire

FIREMEN ON LADDER BATTLE FLAMES IN MIDTOWN BUILDING

Smoke Billows from Glassy Facade onto 46th St. off Madison

Journal-American Photo by Paul Rice

Five minutes of horror . . . and seconds away from death.

Seven persons who tried to get out of a "frying pan" fix were literally trapped in the fire.

The flames erupted yesterday on the fourth floor of a glass-aluminum office building at 20 E. 46th st., off Madison ave.

Dense smoke billowed up air ducts and the elevator shaft to the 14th floor where seven were working.

They rushed to an elevator and started down.

Just as they reached the floor—where the flames were eating through the walls—the elevator stopped.

The blaze had burned out the electric power cables that operate the elevator.

FIREMEN ON HAND

In another elevator was Fireman Robert Post, 31, of Ladder Co. 4. He broke open the door with an axe.

Then, he and Fireman Paul Geidel smashed their way into the other elevator.

Fireman Geidel carried an unconscious woman down four flights of stairs to the street. The other passengers, all men, were led down the stairs.

Those rescued were given oxygen for smoke inhalation and taken to Bellevue Hospital.

12

FORGOTTEN WAR

1952/1953

Enjoy these images I took during my combat tour with the 17th Bomb Wing, 95th Bomb Squadron at both K-1 and K-9 Air Force Bases in Pusan, South Korea.

B-26 waiting combat mission over North Korea at K-1 AFB, Pusan, Korea.

95th Bomb Squadron B-26 at K-1 AFB, Pusan, Korea. Note Squadron logo donkey kicking ass.

95th Bomb Squadron flight line @ K-1 AFB, Pusan, Korea. 1952.

One of two take off wrecks in January 1953 at K-9 AFB. This B-26 was with the 34th Bomb Squadron. The navigator was killed instantly while riding in the nose.

Second take off crash was a B-26 from the 37th Bomb Squadron with no injuries,

Bomb away over North Korea. Mig and F-86 vapor trails seen in back ground.

B-26 taking off to Harm's Way North Korea night mission.

B-26 off to Harm's Way 1953.

Day light formation combat mission, target North Korean airfield. 100% coverage hitting target.

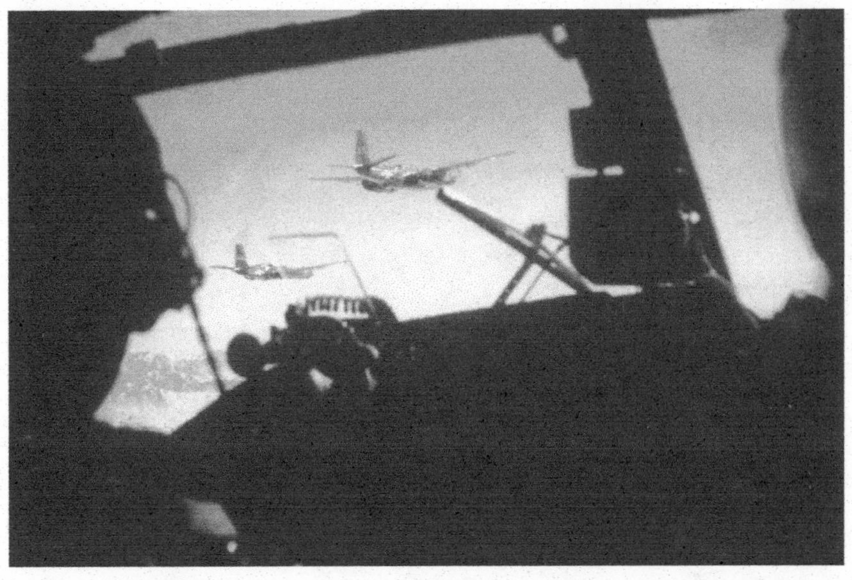

B-26 formation returning home from combat mission.

B-26 Lady Nan of the 95th Bomb Squadron off to Harms Way North Korea.

B-26 instrument panel.

Harm's Way

Me and gunner Sgt. Bill Napier taking a leak at outside urinal.

Gunner Sgt. Paul E. Geidel shown with B-26's 95th Bomb Squadron Kicking Ass Squadron logo.

Mister Nasty snow took over 95th Bomb Squadron flight line. February 1953.

Home of the Black Knights, K-9 AFB, 17th Bomb Wing, Pusan, Korea, 5th Air Force, USAF.

One of the best pilots I flew with, Major Cox is left of me, on right me with my trusted 1911 Colt 45 cal.

I am looking at the 95th Bomb Squadron logo Kicking Donkey kicking ass.

95 Bomb Squadron sign with me.

17th Bomb Wing Bomb dump.

Loading top twin 50 caliber turret with my neckless of 50 caliber bullets,

Bombs away over rugged mountains in North Korea.

L/R Captain George Vioex (pilot), Captain Tom Cameron (bombardier/navigator), A/1C Paul Geidel (gunner). Photo taken after finishing our last combat mission over North Korean.

My brother Richard congratulating me on my safe return and last combat mission. He took leave from front lines where is was stationed to see me.

13

WONDER DRUG 22ND AND 23RD FIRE

1966

Oct. 17th, 1966 at 9:36 Monday night, fire alarm box 598 was transmitted. Address, 21st and Broadway, Manhattan, NYC. Ladder Company's, Engine Company's and Rescue Company 1 (R-1), FDNY respond. Upon arrival R-1 was directed to 7 east 22nd street. The building was involved with extreme heat and smoke. R-1 forced entry into the first floor, and began making a search to locate fire while venting the front of building. The fire located in a basement of a picture frame manufacturing company. R-1 had not yet located the fire. A second alarm was transmitted. Company's arriving on the second alarm stretched hand lines into the first floor and basement of a drug store located at 6 east 23rd street.

This was the "Wonder Drug" store located directly behind 7 east 22nd street. The basement depth of the drug store was shorter than the depth of the first floor. The first floor extending beyond the basement wall and over the basement of the building behind it, 7 east 22nd street, which was fully involved with fire. There was extreme heat and smoke in the drug store. Suddenly the floor broke under the firefighters plunging them into the basement, a flaming cauldron immediately plugged by tons of debris. The fire now extending into the drug store.

The time now was 10:12 PM. Nine firefighters including members of Rescue Co. 1 on the 22nd street side were pinned momentarily in the basement when the wall collapsed. They crawled their way back to the safety of the street. As I recall, R-1 members, Captain Joe Rooney, Firefighters Joe Reres, Joe Duffy, Phil Prial, Ray O'Conner and two others, I don't remember their names were lucky to get out alive. FF Reres temporarily losing his helmet and his hair being singed. Picture'd carrying a fallen fighter, left Joe Reres and right Joe Duffy.

Seven of the nine that were pinned were taken to Bellview Hospital. A third, fourth, and fifth alarm were transmitted as the fire raged out of control.

At 2:45 AM the bodies of two firemen were carried out of the rear of the drug store. Then a second flare up and everyone was ordered out of the building. Firemen still pouring water from inside the storefronts yelled occasional warnings to each other as flames surged up momentarily, leaving the building only to return.

I arrived at the fire scene around 9:15 AM the follow morning. Two more firefighter bodies were recovered hours after the first two were discovered. Six remained missing, buried in tons of debris . At one point during the search, Chief of Dept. John O'Hagen ordered everyone out of the buildings. He wanted to bring in a wrecking ball and knock the rest of the buildings down to make the recovery safer. At the same moment a firefighter said he thought he saw a boot inside the drug store in the debris. Chief O'Hagen, then ordered members of Rescue Co. 1 back into the building to make another search.

It has been years ago so I don't remember exactly who it was we found first. As we dug through tons of debris we located a fallen firefighter. I clearly remember as we recovered him, part of another firefighter's turnout gear was made visible. It was almost like the six missing were holding hands. As we dug and moved debris we were able to recover all the missing one by one. I remember some of the names we recovered, Firefighter Tepper , Battalion Chief Higgins, and Probationary Firefighter Rey. Rey was the last one we located. Firefighter John Driscoll, R-1 was with me when we located Rey.

Rey was buried vertically and it took about an hour getting him out. Driscoll then looked up at me and asked, "are there any more Paul,?" I said "no John, we got them all." I can remember to this day that John started to cry. Sixteen hours after the fire was reported the last of the firefighters were brought out. The time 1:48 PM the next day. It was an honor to be a part of bringing these men home.

14

FALSE ALARM POLE

1964

During a hot summer in 1964, Rescue Co. 1, (R-1) FDNY, 530 W. 43rd St., between 9th and 10th Avenues in Manhattan, was experiencing an unusual amount of false alarms. One alarm box was being pulled much more frequently than any of the others in the area. All fire alarm boxes activated, from 23rd Street to 59th Street, west of 5th Avenue were assigned to R-1. As I recall, this one alarm box located near W. 24th St. and 10th Ave. was activated numerous times that it was decided that it should be placed under police surveillance. Well, that didn't work!

Under the protection of darkness, the alarm box was pulled over and over again during different hours and on different nights. How could this occur as the police had seen no one even near the alarm box? The alarm box was also rechecked for malfunctions and found in excellent condition.

Then the mystery was resolved. On a dark, rainy night the police surveillance noticed a long pole slowly extending out of a nearby building window. As the pole continued extending out of the window, rain was wetting the top of it. A nearby street light reflected brightly off the wet pole, making it clearly visible as it continued to get longer and longer, nearing the alarm box. A small hook attached to the end of the pole gave the person on the other end the ability to pull the alarm box handle, thus transmitting an alarm. As soon as the alarm was sent, the pole quickly disappeared out of sight into the building.

Fire companies arrived and the law breakers were arrested by the police. As a result the percentages of false alarms were quickly reduced in the area.

I might add it was not unusual to arrive at a false alarm only to find out that the alarm box been set on fire!!

What a crazy world we live in. Who does this???

15

THE KING AND I

1954-2008

I began my fast pitch softball by catching with my brother Richard just before joining the United States Air Force. He would practice throwing the ball for about 30 minutes and then rest. I would practice pitching back to him during his break, learning the art of throwing the ball underhand with a windmill delivery. This would go on all summer long and then I left for the Air Force in November 1951.

After flying 43 combat missions over North Korea as a gunner on a Douglas B-26 attack bomber, I was stationed at Walker Air Force base in Roswell, New Mexico and transferred to various Air Force bases, in Cheyenne, Wyoming and then to Amarillo, Texas. I practiced fast pitching during the summer months and whenever I could find a catcher. When I was assigned to a squadron at Amarillo Air Force Base, I decided to join the squadron team and a team in the city of Amarillo.

Pictured below is my first fast pitch softball team. I am at the bottom right corner. Our team won the Amarillo fast pitch league and the playoff championships that year.

During my first season with this team I had the pleasure of meeting the legendary Eddie Feigner of "The King and His Court." He was playing against an all star team from the Amarillo fast pitch league. I had heard of the King and His Court, but never saw this team play.

I was amazed how hard he threw a softball and made it rise. Eventually, I got the courage to walk over to him and question him about how he was able to throw the rise ball and how he held it in his hand.

Eddie took the time to show me. He showed me how to hold then release the ball the right way with my fingers. I tried without success while with him, but I knew with practice I would master it. The days when I was off work, and could get a catcher, I threw the ball at least a hundred pitches a day. Finally, I caught on and every once in awhile the ball would rise. The more I practiced the easier it got for me to throw the rise ball. Next step was learning to control that rise ball.

At one of my local squadron softball games I was scheduled to pitch the game. My catcher said to me, "why don't we try the rise pitch you have been working on?" I had never tried it in a game before and I said, "OK lets give it a try." After warm up, I was on the mound ready to pitch the game. The catcher gave the signal for the rise ball. He didn't change any of his calls, always a rise ball. Actually, all I was able to pitch was a straight fast ball and a slight drop. So, the rise ball was the only pitch I threw during the game.

If I was able to get it near the strike zone, the batter usually swung and missed. I was elated. I had never expieranced anything like this before. I walked more then the nine I had struck out, but striking out nine batters was a high for me as the start of my new fast pitch softball career.

I was on a roll, having fun, and knew as long as I practiced each and everyday I would only get better, making the ball rise faster and with better control. I owe my softball career to Eddie Feigner, the King, he made the following fifty five years in this sport more enjoyable than I ever imagined.

In 1965 I was pitching for the Meade Street Aces out of Perth Amboy, New Jersey and if it wasn't for Eddie Feighner this newspaper clipping below would never have happened.

Point Terrace, Hoboken. PA EN Oct. 22, 65

WITH NOVEMBER just around the corner, the Meade St. Aces softball team of Perth Amboy has decided to hang up the spikes for the season. It was one of the best. The Aces finished with a 54-5-1 record and captured the Perth Amboy City League and Edison Fast-Pitch League and playoff crowns. Paul Geidel was the No. 1 hurler with a near-perfect, 20-1 record and an amazing 231 strikeouts in 166 innings. Included in his collection of wins were 10 shutouts, four one-hitters and five two-hitters. Bill McDermott had a 17-1 record while Dempsey Havrilla turned in an 11-2 mark for Bud O'Donnell's club.

16

BROADWAY CENTRAL HOTEL COLLAPSE

1973

On August 3, 1973, after being off duty for seventy two hours, I started my shift as the Lieutenant assigned to Rescue Company 1, responding to the Broadway Central Hotel. Three days prior, this famous hotel collapsed into ruins killing four people.

Upon arrival, we learned that, although extensive searching was being done, no victims were recovered.

The Deputy Chief, at the scene, questioned me as to where I thought we should start looking. It was his first day there, as well as mine. I guess he must have thought that I had numerous experience with this sort of disaster. I looked up at the pile, taking quite a bit of time observing where to start looking for remains, if any. After my observation, I pointed to an area saying, "I believe we should start there." I sent Firefighter Bobby Burns to that spot.

Then I had a large grappler, which was at the scene, start to dig exactly where I pointed. After the first dig, and only a few minutes later, FF Burns yelled, "we have a body!" The victim's bald head was showing. He was buried vertically, packed solid with debris around his body. We dug around him for numerous hours before we could remove him from the hole.

Once removed, we placed him in a coffin that was at the scene. (Pictured are members of Rescue Company 1 pulling the body from his grave and placing him in a pine coffin. I am, with my helmet, second from the right, deep in hole).

After working for hours, digging the victim out from the debris, the New York Police, in their spit shined shoes and spotless, clean uniforms decided to climb onto the pile and take over.

The NYPD officer in charge insisted that his officers would handle it from here. He stood firm with his reasoning, that he didn't want any complaints about money ever stolen from this victim.

I told him to "fuck off, the victim is naked and R-1 will handle the recovery till the end. We were not in the business of stealing money!"

Only then, did they realize that they did not

have any opportunity to be there. Reluctantly, they left the scene, still as clean as they first arrived.

On the street with their television cameras, waiting for interviews, were hundreds of reporters.

Gabe Pressman, a famous reporter, approached me for an interview. He questioned me. "How were you able to find the first victim so fast? What made you pick that spot from the enormous pile?"

Since the interview was live, I had to be careful with my explanation. I tried delicately as I could, telling the truth.

"I saw a swarm of flies all centered in one spot. It has been hot, over 90 degrees for days since the collapse, the body would be ripe attracting flies. I saw the flies and knew where we should start to dig hoping to find victims."

I am hard-pressed to believe that Gabe Pressman wasn't too pleased with my response. However, this was the truth. It worked for me. The victim's family had their loved one to put to rest!! Hopefully with some closure.

17

MY BABY IS INSIDE

1971

It was a beautiful sunny, summer day in Brownsville, Brooklyn, NY. I was the covering Lieutenant with the 44th Battalion, FDNY, located on Watkins Ave., just off Pitkin Ave. I was assigned to cover a vacation spot for a month, working with Ladder Company 120 (L 120).

During this time period, fire companies in this area were the busiest in the world. Some responding to over 10,000 alarms in a year!

An alarm came in that L-120 was first due, meaning first to arrive. Upon arrival, a one story, unattached, private home was on fire. Smoke and flames were spewing from the rear windows. An engine company arrived before us, stretching a hand line to the rear of the building.

A woman on the street was screaming uncontrollably, "My baby is inside!!!"

A Firefighter from L-120, and I immediately went through an open, front door and started a search of the floor, looking for the baby.

Heavy, thick, black smoke was blowing out the door over our heads. Not wearing Scott Air Packs, we stayed very low, our face about six inches from the floor, as we crawled into the building.

Visibility at this level was clear. We could see completely across the room into the next room. However, we saw no one.

Hearing screams coming from the next room I crawled towards them keeping my face close to the floor.

The engine company that arrived stretched a hose line along the outside of the building to the rear, rather than right through the front door. When they opened up with water, knocking down fire, they pushed heat and smoke throughout the building. At that point, I could feel heat buildup over my head!!!

I crawled to the room where the screams were heard, but saw no one. The screams were right next to me. I thought to myself, "what the fuck, where are these people???"

Looking up through the smoke, I could see a TV. The volume was loud and people could be heard fighting and yelling. The voices on the TV had drawn me into a serious situation. I immediately reversed direction and crawled back to the front door yelling to the firefighter with me to follow, and get out.

We both made it out to the safety of the front yard!

The engine company had advanced their hose line through the rear entrance, knocking down all visible fire in the kitchen, as well as the rest of the building. The fire was brought under control in a matter of minutes.

The baby inside was later reported to be the woman's dog!

Unknown to her, the dog was already safely outside.

This was not the first time people on a street would yell that their baby was trapped inside a burning building. Their baby, more often than not, was a pet

During my firefighting career this was the first and only time, voices on a TV got me in a dangerous situation.

18

BROOKLYN WILDAY RESCUE

January 7, 1976

I was the officer working in Rescue Co. 1 the morning of January 7, 1976. A five alarm fire was raging in a supermarket in Brooklyn. Rescue Co. 1 was special called to the fire in Brooklyn. Upon arrival I split the company into two teams to search for reported missing firefighters.

The fire was located in the large basement of a A&P Supermarket. With my team, each of us wearing Scott Air Packs and tied to a life line entered the basement. It appeared most of the fire had been knocked down by advancing hand lines. However, there was extreme heat and heavy smoke which made the search almost impossible to handle. Because of these conditions, we crawled low on our hands and knees through hallways feeling for any fallen firefighter. Thankfully, our search came up clean, finding no one.

Firefighter Wilday who was searching in a different area climbed down a ladder into the basement. Earlier it was reported two firefighters had fallen through a partially collapsed floor. After an exhaustive search, Firefighter Wilday located both and managed to bring them to safety.

In another area of the basement, members of Rescue Co. 2, located Firefighter Charles Sanchex of Ladder Co. 131. Sadly, he had died in the fire. Another New York City Firefighter lost in the line of duty! I thought to myself will this ever end?

It was not unusual for a rescue company to respond to another borough in the city during multiple alarm fires.

I am pictured below congratulating Wilday for his rescue of the two firefighters,

Lt. Paul Geidel of Tottenville, right, congratulates Fireman Robert Wilday of Great Kills after he rescued two men trapped in the basement of a burning supermarket in Brooklyn.

S.I. Advance Photo by John R. Bessone

Island fireman pulls 2 buddies from fire

By JANICE KABEL

A Great Kills fireman yesterday rescued two of his colleagues from a five-alarm blaze in Brooklyn in which one other fireman died.

Robert (Don) Wilday of 5 Rhett Ave., a 16-year veteran of the Fire Department, rescued the two men from the basement of a burning A&P supermarket at 173 Atlantic Ave. shortly after they had fallen through a partially collapsed floor.

Wilday, assigned to Rescue Co. 1 in Manhattan, brought the two men out about 7 a.m. by crawling down a ladder into the smoky basement. Although he was wearing an air tank, he was not using the mask at the time. "The visibility was bad enough so I didn't put the damn thing on. I wasn't thinking about getting smoke in my eyes, I was thinking about getting those guys out," Wilday said later.

He was given oxygen at the scene and released.

Another Staten Island fireman, Raymond Dunne of 21 Constant Ave., Westerleigh, was saved from the burning building by firefighters.

Dunne was admitted to Long Island College Hospital for treatment of smoke inhalation. He is assigned to Ladder Co. 131 in Brooklyn.

Also on the scene was Lt. Paul Geidel of 20 Parker St., Tottenville, also of Rescue Co. 1, who said that Wilday would be recommended for a departmental citation for heroism. It will be his fourth in seven years with the rescue company.

The dead fireman, pulled out from another corner of the building by firemen from another rescue company more than two hours later, was identified as Charles R. Sanchez, 32, of Ladder Co. 131. In

(Continued on Page 14)

19

FRIDAY THE 13TH

January 13, 1953

In the summer of 1952 during combat crew training at Langley Air Force Base, Virginia, I became a close friend of Airman Dariel Davis from Ada, Oklahoma. We both were training as gunners on the Douglas B-26 Invader, a three men combat crew which consisted of a pilot, navigator/bombardier, and a gunner.

Before being shipped out to Korea we were sent home for a month long vacation, then assigned to a two week survival training course at Stead Air Force Base in Reno, Nevada. The training at Stead consisted of ways to survive if in the event of being forced down in remote and/or unfriendly terrain, how to escape capture, and how to escape if captured.

At Stead Air Force Base we were taught survival techniques, such as fishing, making a rock oven, meat jerky and snare traps. We also were briefed on an imitation combat mission before being sent out on a ten day, twenty mile trek through Plumas National Forest and mountains in Nevada. We were to assume the position that we had survived parachuting from this mission and from there make it safely out of enemy territory.

At Stead Air Force Base personnel were trained to capture and interrogate the fallen and gather as much information as possible about their mission. My crew took all necessary measures not to get captured. However, in the event we were captured, we were instructed to give only our name, rank and serial number.

Putting a capture to the test, we were told our squadron was stationed in Seattle, Washington. There were three squadrons of B-26 aircraft, sixteen in each squadron. We were to take off from Seattle, Washington at a designated time, fly south and bomb targets in San Diego, California. We also were taught to never carry a wallet, family pictures or personal information on a mission as the enemy could use this information against us.

During the twenty mile trek through the mountains and forest, my crew traveled slowly and cautiously. We evaded capture and successfully made it to our pick-up point.

Consequently, my friend, Dariel was not so lucky. He was captured the first week during his twenty mile trek. Later, when we reunited, he told me he was asked all kinds of questions. The enemy even had his wallet! At first Dariel refused to answer any questions other than giving his name, rank, and serial number.

He told me that because he refused to answer their questions, he was put in a pine box placed under a slowly dripping faucet. The sound of each drop would echo loudly as it hit the top of the box. This torture went on for many, many hours without any food or water. To make matters worse, the enemy cooked steaks nearby!! The smell of the cooking steaks would leak through small holes that were drilled in the pine box.

Dariel told me that he was going nuts listening for hours to the constant sound of the dripping faucet. Very slowly "Drip..........drip...........drip", maybe thirty seconds between each drip as the sound echoed inside the box. This practice was a sort of sociological torture. He said he was starting to crack because of hunger and the smell of the juicy steaks cooking!! He couldn't take it anymore so he beat on the box until they released him.

The fear of having to go back in the pine box was so overwhelming that during his interrogation he gave the enemy whatever information they demanded. He told them everything, such as where our mission took off from, where we were bombing, how many planes there were in each squadron. He even told them of his family in Ada, Oklahoma!! What a lesson we all learned from Dariel. We all got a good laugh!!

Eventually we got our orders, and shipped out to Korea together. We were assigned to the 17th Bomb Wing at K-1 Air Force Base, Pusan, Korea. Hopefully, we were all smarter in how to handle a capture in the event we were shot down.

Dariel was assigned to the 37th Bomb Squadron while I was assigned to the 95th Bomb Squadron.

In hardly any time, each of us accumulated many night combat missions. At one point, we flew together on a daylight combat mission which included both the 37th and the 95th Bomb Squadrons. It was a daylight formation consisting of about twelve aircraft headed to an enemy airfield in North Korea. Once over the target we flew a very tight formation to make certain our bomb drop were more effective.

We had a fighter escort and no enemy aircraft was sighted in the area. Photos of the bomb drop taken on our mission confirmed that we had covered 100% of the target area.

In January, on Friday the 13th, Dariel and I spent the afternoon taking pictures of each of our squadron's B-26's. The photo below shows Dariel and I standing behind a B-26.

We were both scheduled for a combat mission that night. However, after returning from my mission I learned that Dariel was killed in action. The loss of my dear friend still haunts me to this day!

Date of Loss:	530113
Tail Number:	44-34546
Aircraft Type:	B-26B
Wing or Group:	17th Bmb Wg (L)
Squadron:	37th Bmb Sq (L)
Circumstances of Loss:	Crashed into the sea about 2 miles off end of runway after take-off from Pusan

Crewmembers Associated With This Loss				
Name (Last, First Middle)	Rank	Service	Status	Comments
BAUWIN, Eugene E.	CAPT	USAF	NBD	
DAVIS, Dariel L.	A2C	USAF	NBD	
HALL, Harlan P.	2LT	USAF	NBD	

I continued flying night combat missions, with Dariel always in my prayers. Once I finished my tour of duty, I returned to the United States, and was stationed at Roswell Air Force Base in Roswell, New Mexico. I was assigned to the famous 509th Bomb Wing, 393rd Bomb Squadron as a gunner on a B-29. This was Colonel Paul Tibbets outfit, famous for dropping the atomic bomb "Little Boy" August 6th 1945 on Hiroshima, Japan.

In early November 1954, I wrote Dariel's wife a letter telling her of the many pictures I had of him. I asked her if she would like to have them. Below, is the letter I received before I sent her pictures of Dariel. However, to this day, I never heard from her again.

November 3, 1951

Dear Mr. Geidel,

I received your letter yesterday. I certainly do appreciate your writing me as I would like very much to have the pictures of Daniel. Although I remarried a short time ago, I still want them because I have a very sweet little girl that is Daniel's and I want her to have all the things possible that she might have some idea, someday, as to who her daddy was. She is the very image of Daniel and I am so proud of her.

I wish to thank you in advance for being so nice as to send me the pictures.

Sincerely,
Jawanna Davis Guest
208 S. Hope Ave.
Ada, Oklahoma

20

TOP FLOOR FIRE

1974

I was the officer working on a hot, summer, night tour with Rescue Co. 1, FDNY in Manhattan, responding to an all hands fire on the lower east side of Manhattan. The fire was on the top floor of a five story tenement building in alphabet city. (Ave's A, B, C). While we were on our way, a second alarm was transmitted. The progress reported over the radio, was that the fire was doubtful will hold, and the top floor was completely involved with fire.

Note: Exposures #1, a street, # 2 a similar type building, #3 a rear yard and #4 a similar type building.

Upon arrival, looking up, you could see the top floor was fully involved. Fire was visibly blowing out of all front, floor windows. Ladder Co. 11 was at the scene, in front of the building

Engine companies were advancing on the fire with two hand lines from the interior of the building.

Our orders were to give a primary search of the building, getting everyone out, and open up the roof. I sent two of my men to the roof via exposure 2. The rest of us went into the fire building, searching for any victims still inside.

The Ladder Company 11 was setting up their ladder pipe, ready to pump water into the building at 1,000 gallons a minute; a lot of weight, as water weighs about 8 1/3 lbs. a gallon. Also, two hand lines delivering 250 gallons a minute out of a 2 1/2 inch hose added to the weight.

As water is pumped into a building, it also needs a place to leave. The possibility of a building collapse is always a threat to the lives of firefighters when so many gallons of water are being pumped into a structure, the weight sometimes it just won't hold. Again, water needs a place to escape, whether cascading down a stairway or out the front or rear doors.

The top floor was gutted. Water that was being put on the fire was filtering down through out, flooding the floors below. Eventually, the fire was put under control.

Most companies were ordered to take up. However, we needed to make our primary search of the floors below looking for any possible victims or fire extension.

During our search in one of the apartments, we found a man sitting on his couch watching TV in his pajamas. There appeared to be very little smoke condition, but his apartment had about six (6) inches of water throughout.

He was pissed off, calling us "white trash" as well as other words.

I told him we were not white trash, we're only there to help and that he had to leave the building.

He shouted that he was going nowhere, calling us "mother fuckers", ordering us to get rid of the water in his apartment and then get the fuck out!

I figured okay. Let's help this prick!!

I ordered my ax man, Firefighter Jessy Bilboa to start cutting a hole in the center of his living room floor. Jessy swung the blade of his ax like Paul Bundy or a tree surgeon. After about six accurate swings of his ax he got a nice size hole. Water started swirling down the hole!

I will never forget the look on the man's face.

"There," I said, "the water problem will be over in a little while. Now, go fuck yourself, you ungrateful piece of shit! Get out of the building."

He never said another word as he grabbed a jacket, leaving his apartment while walking through the water soaked floor.

We continued our search of the entire building, finding no one. We were ordered to take up and never heard another word about what happened.

Note: In some cases, buildings that are on fire, storing large bails of fabric, paper, or other absorbent material, water can't escape easily. A weight problem escalates if the fire cannot be brought under control quickly. The possibility of a collapse becomes very real!

21

THE NIGHT I WEPT

February 15, 1968

While working a night tour February 15th 1968 (6 PM to 9 AM) with Rescue Company 1, Fire Department New York, a fire alarm was transmitted from Park Avenue and 42nd Street. Rescue Company 1 was quartered with Engine Company 65, located on 43rd Street between 5th & 6th Avenues, Manhattan, NY. Both companies responded.

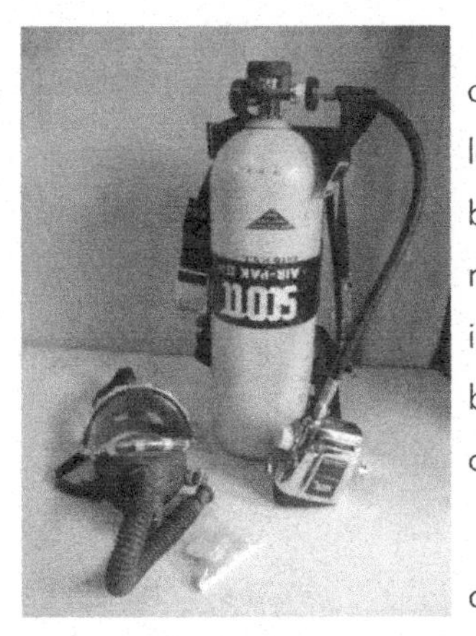

Upon arrival, fire was spewing from the windows on the third floor of Rudley's Coffee Shop, located on the first floor of the old four story brick building, sandwiched between two modern high rise buildings. A woman on the street was screaming uncontrollably, "My two little girls are still in the building! My babies, my babies!" She was frantically crying, clasping both hands against her face.

I donned a Scott Air Pack and immediately climbed the front fire escape to the third floor. (The Scott Air Pack is similar to a scuba divers equipment, allowing the wearer approximately thirty minutes of pure breathing air). Two, of the three, third floor windows lead to the fire escape, the third a long fall to the street! I proceeded to firmly place the Scott front piece on my face, tighten the straps and check for leaks.

While putting on my leather gloves, I dropped the right one, losing it off the fire escape. I then ducked under flames which were coming out the first window going to the middle window. With my ax, I took out the glass and supporting mullions. Fire immediately came out from above. Ducking under the flames, I climbed into the burning room, making a quick search, while at the same time calling for anyone in the room. The room was completely involved with flames! The heat intensified and was unbearable! I dove out the same window, back onto the fire escape.

Engine Co. 65 had stretched their hose line up the fire escape and were starting to get water on the fire. Firefighter Ken Horner, of E-65, saw me dive out the window onto the fire escape. I yelled to him, "Wet me down, wet me down, my hand and knees are burning!" Ken quickly turned the water on me to stop the burning. Then he turned and started knocking down all visible fire at the window in front of him and continued to knock down all fire in the room I just dove out of.

I then went back through the first window to make a search. I located a couch and on the couch huddled close together were the two little girls burned beyond recognition. At this point, I completely lost it! I wept! I got there too late to save them!

Afterwards, I was taken to a nearby hospital for treatment in the emergency room. I heard coming from a radio a firefighter being interviewed. He spoke about the fire and the two little girls losing their lives. He mentioned my name and another firefighter who claimed he went in the window with me. Since I went in alone, I asked myself, "Who was this other person?" The bullshit was starting to hit the fan.

After I was treated at the hospital for burns on my right hand, knees and ears, I returned to the firehouse, prior to being placed on medical leave. While there, a member told me it was he that yelled "dive out this window!" (If I had dove out the third window, I would have landed on the street). I said to him, "I didn't hear anyone yelling anything to me."

Still puzzled about the radio interview, I wanted to know why this member claimed we both went into the window and found the little girls. I asked him and his answer was feeble, claiming that Ladder Company 2 was going to take credit for finding the little girls. Puzzled, I decided to just drop the subject.

Firefighter Ken Horner later told me that the Deputy Chief in charge had asked him if he had seen me go through the burning window, into the building.

Horner said, "No." The Chief immediately replied sarcastically, "I didn't think so." Horner replied back to the Chief, "but I saw him come out!" Silence from the Chief. (All this you hear after the fire is out.)

However, no one knew what was about to happen!! This is where it gets very interesting.

The one star edition of the New York Daily News is now out on the streets. On the front page, is a full page picture of me diving out of the third floor window onto the fire-escape showing the fire clearly around me. During the day, the two star, three star, four star and the five star edition of the paper came out. Each edition with the same picture of me on the front page. Firefighter Ken Horner was shown getting water on the fire in the first window. Other firefighters who claimed to be close to me, are not pictured by my side!

I asked myself, "What were they thinking? Why all the story telling?"

Since the building next to Rudley's Coffee Shop was a high rise, and the headquarters of the New York Daily News, one of their photographers was on the street and able to shoot the photo of me just as I bailed out of the flaming window. Confucius say, "One picture worth a thousand words".

At the firehouse the bull shitters remained quiet. What could they say? It's my guess if it weren't for the picture, the truth would never have come out.

My burns healed. I went off medical leave and ordered back to work.

In the firehouse this subject was never mentioned again. Everything was forgiven. We had work to do.

Rudley's
coffe
sho
2 Little Girls Die in 42d St. Fire

Hot job needs cool head

By PETER REICH

Smoke fills the room, the fire roars over the din of sirens — and Fireman Paul Geidel of Tottenville moves carefully and deliberately through the smoke, seeking possible victims.

A veteran of 11 years of rescue work, Geidel is one of eight Staten Islanders in Manhattan's Rescue Co. 1.

The company drills daily to keep in shape for "that one situation."

The situation happened last Thursday when the company was called only a few blocks from its 43rd St. headquarters to a fire in an apartment building on 42nd St., in which two children perished.

Once in a fire, says Geidel, "you use your training and skill for one daring try." That one try — which failed Thursday but which has helped him to rescue persons from burning buildings, smoke-filled, jammed elevators and window ledges — is not a haphazard, heroic gesture. Several basic ground rules, he points out, keep rescue firemen alert and safety-conscious.

The main rule is to keep oriented. If you know where you came in, you'll know where to get out.

Your ears are your thermostat. (Geidel's ears were singed Thursday.) They tell you how hot it is and where the fire is burning.

A tool such as an ax kept in front of you warns of dangerous shafts and a weakened structure.

You move deliberately and carefully along walls. Walls lead to windows, and windows provide exits. Frequently, persons collapse near windows. Following a wall also helps keep a fireman oriented.

Last week's fire was not unusual, notes Geidel. "There have been a lot of fatal fires recently, with more parents being saved than kids. Parents aren't staying with their children."

Often, when firemen find children, they were left alone or weren't taken from the building when the fire started.

When do fires start? "They come mostly around mealtime," observes Geidel, "especially when one of the boys (at the firehouse) brings something good his wife cooked."

Moving fast and hitting hard are not just a part of Geidel's profession. During a hitch with the Air Force, he was an aerial gunner on [illegible] missions during the Korean War. A [illegible] fan of fast-pitch softball, he looks forward to playing Double-A softball in the Perth Amboy-New Brunswick League this spring.

The fireman lives at [illegible] Sleight Ave. with his wife Pat, and four children.

Fireman Paul Geidel tells his family how he received a burned hand while trying in vain to save two Manhattan girls in a fire. Left to right, are Michael, 5; Gary, 11; Mrs. Geidel, and Ralph, 9.

S.I. Advance Photo by Robert J. Parsons

How 2 Children Perished in Fire

By CY EGAN

A fireman told today of a futile attempt to save two small sisters trapped in a photographer's blazing East Side studio.

"There was just too much heat and flames," said fireman Paul Geidel, 29, of Rescue Co. 1, who arrived at the building at 202 E. 42d St. last night, to find the girls' mother, Mrs. Sheril Studebaker, 20, on the second-floor fire escape landing screaming, "My babies! My babies!"

"She was pointing to the third floor," Geidel said. "I went up and kicked in the windows, climbed inside and made as fast a search as I could. But the heat was terrific. I dove back out. Then they opened up the hose lines. I went in through another window. This time I found the kids, but they were beyond help."

The bodies of the children—Betsy, 3, and Molly, 4 were found huddled on a mattress in the left front corner of the studio owned by Les Underhill, 27.

Blaze Spread Rapidly

Underhill and his wife, Eva, 20, who live in Barnegat, N. J., and Mrs. Studebaker and her husband, James, 21, recently employed as Underhill's assistant, were in a fourth-floor studio operated by Jack Horner, of Hicksville, L. I., when the fire started, police said.

"I went to get my flashlight to see where the fire was," Horner said. "We knew the children were on the third floor. We made every effort to get them.

"But the smoke was so black you couldn't breathe. The flames spread amazingly fast. Within a few seconds, it became a matter of saving your own life—honestly, it was that bad."

Horner escaped uninjured down an aerial ladder from the top floor of the five-story building. The Studebakers and Mrs. Underhill later were treated for shock at Bellevue, where Underhill was treated for burns of the left arm. Another photographer, Arnold Borget, of 610 West End Av., was admitted to the hospital with hand and face burns.

Police said the Studebakers had been living on Mott St. since coming here from Ohio after the husband was employed by Underhill, an advertising layout photographer.

Fireman Injured

Geidel suffered burns of the head, hands and legs in his rescue attempt. He also was treated at Bellevue.

In another blaze, five drivers and employes suffered burns when gasoline being pumped into a taxi exploded in the one-story Yankee Cab Service garage at 292 E. 139th St., The Bronx, touching off a two-alarm fire early today. All the injured were taken to Jacobi Hospital.

A two-alarm fire in a five-story tenement at 61 E. 123d St. drove about a dozen families to the street in sub-freezing weather shortly after 2 a.m.

22

MAYFLOWER HOTEL

December 27, 1961

December 27, 196l, I reported to Rescue Company 1 for my night tour from six in the evening until nine the following morning. I reported to Lieutenant William McMahon, the officer in charge. After roll call he assigned each of the members their assigned tools and jobs, which consisted of the can man (2 ½ gallon water fire extinguisher) with a six foot hook. An outside vent man, a roof man and a forcible entry team. After being assigned our jobs, we had an hour drill on one of the many tools that Rescue I carried on their rig.

After the drill, we enjoyed our evening meal with the thoughts that we could settle back and enjoy a quiet night hoping that the city people were safely tucked in their beds after a busy Christmas week.

Our wish was short-lived. A fire alarm was transmitted at one fifty seven in the morning coming from the fashionable Mayflower Hotel, which was located on West 61st, and Central Park West, Manhattan. The fire was reported out of control, on the ninth floor of the seventeen story residential hotel. A second alarm was immediately transmitted for Box 22-946.

Members of Engine Company 23 hooked up their hand line to a standpipe on the eighth floor below the fire. Struggling with their water charged 2 ½ inch hose line, the crew advanced from the eighth floor to the ninth floor. At the moment they reached the ninth floor a deadly fireball engulfed the hallway. The fireball killed firefighter John King, 29, and seared four other firefighters with him. The ninth floor apartment of play writer, Murray Wyzel was fully involved in fire. The door to his apartment was wide open thus allowing the fire to spread into the hallway. There was no law in place for apartments to have self-closing hinges on the door.

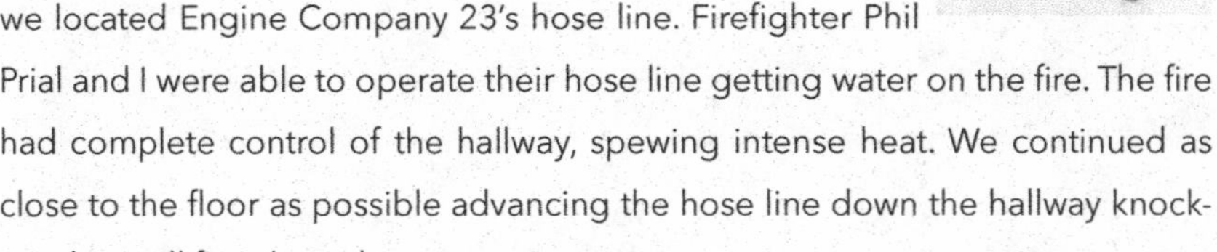

Soon after, the fireball that knocked out Engine Company 23 and the death of Firefighter King, Rescue Co. 1 arrived to the ninth floor, all wearing Scott Air Packs.

Staying low, as close to the floor as possible (six inches), we located Engine Company 23's hose line. Firefighter Phil Prial and I were able to operate their hose line getting water on the fire. The fire had complete control of the hallway, spewing intense heat. We continued as close to the floor as possible advancing the hose line down the hallway knocking down all fire along the way.

We fought our way into the apartment of sixty year old Murray Wyzel, whose apartment was completely involved with fire. Wyzel was found wandering about aimlessly, badly burnt. Once all visible fire was knocked down, Firefighter Prial and I began a primary search of the apartment looking for any other possible victims. Visibility was zero due to the thick heavy black smoke. While making our search we used the wall as a guiding point. I was on one side of the room, Prial on the other. The wall lead us to a huge window opening. The window had been blown out with the sill being only inches from the floor. Tragically, if either of us had lost our balance while leaning on the wall to the window opening we would have fallen nine stories to our death! A factor many firefighters encounter while making a search in a heavy smoke charged room or building.

On the front page of the New York Post, I am pictured on the right, wearing my helmet. The intensity of the heat was so aggressive that it caused my old blue helmet front piece to change to a ghostly white. Firefighter Tom Bonamo, Rescue Company 1, is clearly seen in the rear of the photo.

Behind the Transit Strike Threat

New York Post

LATE CITY

MIDTOWN HOTEL BLAZE KILLS 3

Rescue Company 1 and Rescue Company 3 are seen in the above photo giving CPR to both Firefighter King and to play writer Murry Wyzel, who both perished in the blaze. In the other photo below, members of Rescue Company 1 are pictured carrying Murry Wyzel to an awaiting ambulance. Left to right are pictured Firefighter Lefty Surdokoski, Firefighter Paul E. Geidel, Lieutenant William McMahon and Firefighter Philip Prial, all members of Rescue Company 1.

Within the Fire Department of New York City, the company helmet front pieces are color coded. Firefighters in a Rescue Company are blue with a white number, red are Ladder Companies, black are Engine Companies, green are Marine Companies and yellow are Squad Companies.

The color of the helmet front pieces easily identifies a firefighter at fire scenes showing which company he is assigned.

Enough drama for one night! We returned to quarters hoping the rest of our tour would be without incident and it was.

23

POOR GEORGE

1965

On a cold winter evening, I was a firefighter assigned to Rescue Company 1, FDNY. The officer on duty was Lt. William McMahon, when a fire alarm was transmitted reporting that there was a fire on the third floor of a six-story tenement building. Rescue was not assigned to respond to this alarm.

However, Rescue Company 1 received a call from the dispatcher informing us that there was a burn victim on the third floor of the building and to respond. We immediately responded to the location.

Once there, we carried our first aid equipment and a resuscitator to the third floor. In the hallway, lying just outside a burnt out apartment, was a man, legless from the knees, with about sixty percent of his body burnt badly.

Immediately, we started first aid, applying Americane burn spray on all visible burns; mostly the arms, neck and face. His breathing was labored so I also gave him oxygen from the resuscitator. The man was very upset and he appeared to be very frightened. A normal reaction to his serious injuries.

I asked him, "What is your name?"

He responded, "My name is George. I tried to put out the fire, but it took off quickly."

"George, things will be OK. You should have gotten out of the apartment and let us handle it," I replied.

Again, I repeated so as to comfort him, "you will be just fine, it's all going to be OK."

After we finished covering George's burns with the burn spray, we wrapped him with sterile white sheets a blanket and placed him in our Stokes stretcher. The Stokes stretcher is a metal wire stretcher shaped in the form of a person.

George appeared to settle down and relax. He was very alert, although oblivious to how badly his face was burnt. I'm sure the pain he was encountering was unbearable!

Then the shit hit the fan!!!!!! His wife, Mabel arrived. How she managed to make her way to the fire floor was a mystery.

She approached her husband by standing at the head of the Stokes stretcher looking down at him.

She started screaming loudly, "George, what the fuck did you do? Look at our beautiful apartment! Look at your face! The skin is hanging off your face!!"

George's eyes rolling back as far as he could straining to see her as she stood over his head, looking down at him.

She continued to scream uncontrollably, letting George know how bad his face was burnt and again yelling about the skin that was peeling from his face. She also carried on about all their beautiful furniture that was burnt and how he ruined everything in their apartment! There was nothing left!

The police, who were at the scene, witnessed Mabel yelling at her husband and quickly removed her away and out the door!

George, upset, but straining to see her as she was led away, in a very low garbled voice said, "May, Maay, Maaayble." He then proceeded to choke! He stopped breathing!

I quickly responded to the situation and carefully put the resuscitator rubber mask firmly over his face. Thank God, I got a perfect seal, forcing oxygen into his lungs as another Rescue 1 fire fighter was performing external cardiac massage. We could see his chest rise and fall. Perfect! Hopefully, George will survive. Finally, a doctor arrived. He was quick to say that George wasn't getting oxygen. I knew better and informed the doctor otherwise. Nevertheless, he was the doctor and he had the power to take over.

From the doctor's bag, he pulled out a sharp razor blade. He made a one inch vertical cut into George's esophagus just below the Adams Apple. Immediately after the cutting, oxygen from the resuscitator escaped, thus no longer getting into his lungs!!

Quickly, I took the aspirator part (a short narrow rubber tube) of the resuscitator and placed it back into the cut trying to give George oxygen. Although we continued to work on him for approximately another thirty minutes, we were unsuccessful.

The doctor pronounced him dead of an apparent heart attack. Later, we learned that George had a history of cardiac arrest.

It is my opinion, George died as a direct result of his wife, Mabel's total disregard for his serious burns and knowing full well his prior history of heart attacks. Rescue 1 was able to get George calm and breathing on his own until Mabel went totally nuts and screamed at him! It was just way too much for poor George to handle!

24

31ST STREET FIRE

July 1965

On a sunny summer afternoon, a fire broke out on the third floor of a loft building in mid-town Manhattan, New York City. Rescue Company 1 responded to the fire alarm box located at the intersection of 31st Street and 5th Avenue. Upon arrival fire was visible spewing from the third floor windows of the loft building. As we got off the rig, a chief, who arrived before us, gave an order to immediately search the third and upper floors for anyone that may be trapped.

Donning Scott Air Pak's, Firefighter Martin Cunniff of Rescue Company 1 and I went to the third floor, other members of the company to the upper floors. On the third floor, the heat and smoke was unbearable with no visibility. Staying below the heat level, we proceeded to crawl down a narrow hallway. My flashlight barely shining a beam on the walls.

At this point, Engine Company 65 had advanced a hand line to the third floor. Before they got water, Marty and I got as far down the hallway as we could being met with a wall of fire. Retracing our steps, we retreated back to Engine Company 65. I informed the officer that there was a heavy body of fire down the hallway. After the engine company got water in their line, they advanced down the hallway, knocking down all fire ahead of them. Marty and I followed and located a door in the hallway. We forced open the door and on the other side was a firefighter from Ladder Company 3 standing over an unconscious woman sitting slouched in a chair. The firefighter had come into the room through a window from his aerial ladder and started mouth-to-mouth resuscitation on the woman.

Because of the fire situation, intense heat and smoke, we told the firefighter we would take it from here and carry the woman to the street below. Pictured in a local newspaper is Marty (no helmet) and I carrying her to a nearby ambulance. The other picture to the right shows Marty placing her on a stretcher, my hands show on the right.

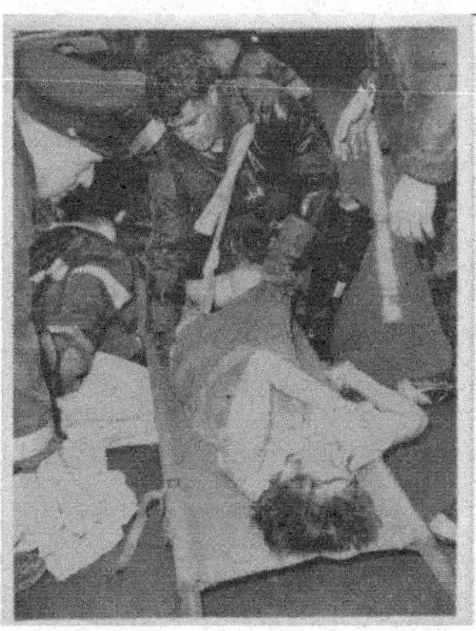

The good news is that with the help of oxygen, the woman regained conscienenes. It felt good that day saving that woman's life. The Ladder Company 3 firefighter deserves all the credit locating her and starting lifesaving procedures.

25

BRONX TELEPHONE EXPLOSION

1962

Even when off duty you answer the call. One afternoon in-between night tours, a few of us from Rescue Company 1 were just hanging out at the firehouse. The date was Oct. 3rd, 1962. A report over the department radio reported that there was an explosion in an office building at 213th St., Manhattan. My Lieutenant, Bill McMahon said lets go. If I remember correctly there were four of us, we grabbed our turnout gear and took a train to the disaster scene. A boiler had exploded in the basement of the New York Telephone Co. building next to a filled cafeteria at lunch time. The boiler went through the wall like a missile killing anything in its path.

When we arrived all fire had been knocked down. There were bodies everywhere throughout the blast area. Many were women, and still missing under desks, twisted metal and concrete. Over twenty people were killed and one hundred injured from the blast. We worked the disaster scene for hours then left to work our night tour back at Rescue 1. I don't remember what happened during our night tour but I'm sure it wasn't quiet.

FINAL 5¢ New York Mirror

95 Hurt, Many Rescued

21 Killed In B'way Phone Office Blast

STORIES ON 2, 3 AND 43. PHOTOS ON PAGES 2, 3, 4, 5 AND CENTER FOLD

Known Dead

26

BROOKLYN 2ND ALARM

March 7, 1970

Not all the fires I responded to were with Rescue Company 1, FDNY. In 1968, I was promoted to Lieutenant out of Rescue Company 1 and assigned to the 44th Battalion, East New York, Bedford-Stuyvesant section of Brooklyn (the Ghetto).

During this time period it was not unusual for fire companies to respond to over 10,000 alarms a year in this area; 60% to 65% of these were false alarms. However, the remaining 35% were more than a very heavy work load for firefighters!

One evening, while I was assigned to Ladder Company 123, an unusual amount of false alarms were transmitted. We responded too many of them.

While out on a false alarm, I received a radio call from the fire department dispatcher telling us to respond to 1342 St. Marks Ave. We were late in getting there. Our time was lost due to the false alarm.

Upon arrival, the building, a 15 foot wide, three story brick was fully involved with fire! The fire was spewing out of the second and third floor windows!

Engine companies arrived at the scene late because they were also responding to false alarms. They quickly stretched hose lines to attack the fire.

Our initial attempt to enter the building was impossible due to the heavy body of fire. However, once the engine company got water and knocked down the fire on the second floor, we were able to make a search for any possible victims.

I knew it was a futile attempt and that no one could possibly survive this inferno. My search to the second floor led me to find a severely burned child lying dead on a bed!

I give enormous credit to the engine company who advanced the line and knocked down all visible fire on the third floor. The heat, flames, and smoke were unbearable.

We continued our search on the third floor, only to find six more dead children! We later found out that a baby sitter had jumped from the third floor and miraculously survived.

Sadly, seven kids were lost because of this fire! If fire company's weren't busy responding to false alarms some of these children might have been saved.

Many of my fire stories are what a firefighter deals with every time he answers that call. These memories will haunt them forever!

When I got home from each tour of duty I made sure to hug my kids and tell them how much I love them.

DAILY NEWS, SATURDAY, MARCH 7, 1970 — 3

Seven Children Die in B'klyn Fire

By RICHARD HENRY

Several small children died and a young woman and her two little girls were injured last night in a fire of unknown cause that devoured a three-story brick building at the border of the Bedford-Stuyvesant and East New York sections of Brooklyn.

John T. O'Hagan, chief of the Fire Department, said after the one-alarm blaze had been brought under control and the children's bodies taken to the Kings County Hospital morgue:

[illegible]

Plagued by Fires

[illegible]

27

GARDEN BRAWL

August 4, 1965

It was the night of August 4, 1965 and all was quiet at Rescue Company 1, located in Engine Company 65's firehouse, at 43rd Street, between 5th & 6th Avenues, mid-town Manhattan. Lieutenant William McMahon was the rescue officer on duty when at 10:50 PM a Class 3 manual fire alarm was transmitted.

A Class 3 fire alarm is a fire alarm transmitted from a box located within a building, not from the street. There is a well-known sign that reads, "In case of a fire, break glass, and pull handle." The little hammer hanging next to it on a small chain.

The Class 3 alarm box that was pulled came from inside Madison Square Garden, located on 8th Ave., between 49th and 50th Streets. R-1 immediately responded. Upon arrival, thousands of people were exiting the Garden. Several hundred were shoving, pushing and fighting one another. The turmoil was unbelievable!!

On that night there was a ten round, non-titled bout between the favorite, Puerto Rican born, Frankie Narvsez, and Filipino junior lightweight champion, Gabriel Elorde. After the decision was announced all hell broke loose. Yelling and fighting erupted. An organ was torn from its mountings in the mezzanine and thrown down into the main lobby. Fire extinguishers, brass railing, axes torn from the wall, loose chairs, seats and beer cans were thrown from the balcony into the crowd below. Complete chaos!!

It did not take long before the fighting continued outside the building onto the streets and nearby subway.

Battalion 9, along with three other fire companies, Ladder Company 4, Engine Company 54 and Rescue Company 1, arrived at the scene, Madison Square Garden. We were huddled together just outside the entrance to the Garden. Thousands of fans rushing from the Garden circled the firefighters. Across the street, there was an old building being demolished. The loose bricks from the building being torn down, were spewed everywhere. Angered fans did not hesitate to pick up the bricks and throw them at anyone within throwing distance. It did not matter if it was police officers, firefighters, or anyone else for that matter.

I was standing next to Firefighter Herbert Peterson of Rescue Company 1, when a thrown brick hit him directly in the mouth! Peterson dropped unconscious to the pavement. He was bleeding profusely, it appeared to me his pallet may have been broken, and many teeth knocked out!!

The Battalion Chief in charge became enraged when Peterson was hit by a brick. He immediately ordered all firefighters to "get those bastards." However, we were surrounded by hundreds of rioters that were threatening us. It was scary but we went on the attack, defending ourselves. Two of the firefighters remained with Peterson, shielding him from more danger, while trying to tend to his injuries.

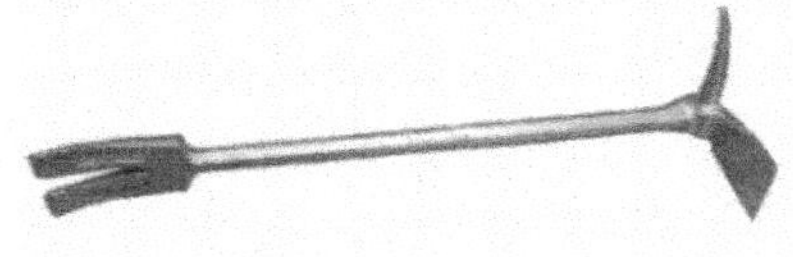

During this chaos, I was carrying an eight pound ax. The others were carrying force-able entry tools (heavy irons) and six foot hooks. My Lieutenant William McMahon was carrying a heavy rechargeable light called a "Wheatlight," a light that Rescue officers carried at the time.

Firefighter Ray Brown, Rescue Company 1 and I squared off with four of the rioters. Ray was carrying a Halligan, (a forcible entry tool made of iron) which he used to defend himself. My defense was the ax handle and back side of the ax head. Just as we were about to mix it up, a mounted police officer seeing this, came galloping though the mob to protect us. He spun his horse around numerous times knocking rioters to the ground while swinging a club. He hit at least four rioters on the head. Ray and I plummeted two different rioters to the ground using our fists and tools. We held them until they were arrested by the police.

Nearby, during the riot, Lieutenant McMahon defended himself with his Wheatlight. He knocked one rioter to the ground with the light, thus earning him the nick name, "Wheatlight Willie." Other firefighters were busy defending themselves against the angry mob. Fists were flying everywhere!!

When the riot first broke out, there were only a few police officers at the scene. Reinforcements were called and within no time seven police cars arrived with three mounted police. It was surprising how quickly the situation was brought under control once more police officers arrived at the scene.

Eventually, we heard that at least nine of the rioters were hospitalized and many more were arrested.

During this tragic situation, Firefighter Peterson was removed from the scene by ambulance and brought to a nearby hospital where he was admitted.

The next morning, our night crew went to the hospital to visit him. But, before visit, I stopped and bought him some get well gifts, thinking it was the least I could do for my friend.

Once we all entered his room, we found him sitting up in his bed. His face bandaged so as that he couldn't speak. However, he brightened up and was very excited to see us as we entered.

Because he could not speak, he had to write his many questions for us to answer on a clipboard. This went on for some time.

After the Q&A, I decided it was time to give him his get well gifts; two ears of corn and a pack of chicklets!

He looked at me with piercing eyes, followed by the middle finger!!!

Then we all had a good laugh as we said our goodbyes!

Lt. Bill McMahon…Wheat Light Willie

Garden's Fight Ends in a Riot Among 7,000

DAILY ALMANAC

FINAL

DAILY NEWS

NEW YORK'S PICTURE NEWSPAPER

7¢

RING FANS RIOT, WRECK GARDEN

Split Verdict Enrages 7,000

28

MISS AMERICA AT THE AMERICANA HOTEL

May 14, 1973

Rescue Company 1 responded to a smoke condition at the women's house of detention in midtown Manhattan. Upon arrival we entered the prison and made a search of the first floor. Many of the women behind bars were yelling sexual offers to us. The smoke condition was from a small fire from a burning newspaper on the first floor.

The chief in charge told us to take up because a call came in for us to respond to the Americana Hotel. It was a short ride responding to the hotel. We went to the upper floors where there was a smoke condition. It turned out this was caused by welders, welding in an elevator shaft at a lower level.

We went to the roof to vent the elevator shaft and BINGO! There were fifty beautiful women in bathing suits, a sash wrapped around of each of them naming which state they represented. They were posing for pictures for the upcoming Miss America pageant.

I am pictured below bighting my tongue, licking my chops at this beautiful contestant! If you look close you will see the shoes of another beauty wrapped around Rescue members. This photo appeared in local tabloids.

Can you imagine!!! We respond to a women's prison in midtown Manhattan, then immediately to the top floor of the prestigious Americana Hotel greeted by fifty of the most beautiful young women in the United States!!!

Firefighters in New York City have such a demanding job, but sometimes we are rewarded!!!

29

A FISH TALE

1972

The year was 1972. It was a very hot summer evening. I was assigned to Squad Company 5, F.D.N.Y., in Chinatown, Manhattan. A fire alarm was transmitted assigning us to be the first to arrive to the scene. We immediately responded to the address reported over the department radio. Upon arrival, we forced entry through the front door of a three story commercial building. We discovered several small fires (15) throughout the first floor. There were candles burning with shredded newspaper around them, waiting to be ignited. It was obvious that it was an arson attempt to burn the building down.

I ordered my forcible entry team to force a door open to another room and make a search, when a loud voice said, "Don't force that door." I responded, "It was my order and I am in charge." "Not any more. I am a Captain and you can take up and get the fuck out of here" he responded.

I was pissed that he, Captain Bourbon of Ladder Co. 18,

insulted me in front of my men, but he was in charge, so I got my men together and took up.

When we returned to our firehouse I told my men we have to get even with this bastard! No way should he have responded to me that way.

I was informed that this Captain had a few more days to go before being promoted to Battalion Chief. I had very little time to get even. He would be transferred somewhere else in the city.

Later, that same night, across from the firehouse, I spotted a large, dead fish lying on the street, next to the curb. With a newspaper in hand I walked across the street and picked up the fish. It must have weighed about twenty pounds!! It was infested with maggots and smelled horrible! Now it was wait-time.

Hours passed. A fire alarm was transmitted from a nearby housing project. Squad 5 and Ladder 18 were both assigned. I had my chance to get even with Captain Bourbon. On the way to the housing project we would be going past Ladder 18's quarters. We responded.

Perfect!!!

Every New York City fire officer carried an alarm box key which opened all fire alarm boxes and locked firehouses throughout the city.

Whenever a fire company was out on a call, the firehouse was vulnerable to thieves who broke in and took whatever they could lay their hands on. Ladder Company 18 had prior problems. So, assigned to their quarters was light duty firefighter recovering from injuries as the security guard. As luck would have it, the light duty firefighter was a member of Squad 5.

Again perfect!

I brought the fish along for the ride.

On the way to the housing project, we stopped at Ladder 18. I gave my trusted firefighter, Willie Williamson my alarm box key and the fish. I told Willie to go upstairs to the Captains office and put the fish in his bed. Also to make sure the maggots were though out the sheets.

Willy unlocked the front door to the firehouse. Within one minute, he did exactly what I asked. However, on the way out the door the security guard who was sleeping saw us. He asked what was going on. I told him, "Go back to sleep, you didn't know anything. You never heard a sound."

We continued to the fire scene. Ladder 18 was already in the building. The alarm was for a smoke condition in an apartment in the building. The Chief in charge ordered me and other companies to take up. We were not needed.

However, I didn't leave the scene too soon. I wanted to make sure Captain Bourbon saw me and the Squad. So I stayed and made brief conversation with the Chief and others, until Bourbon came out and made eye contact with me. Once that happened, it was a go. We took up.

On the way back to our quarters all Squad members, including me, were laughing hysterically imaging the outcome! We were visualizing Bourbon climbing into bed with the rotted fish and maggots.

Once we returned to quarters, I climbed into bed, smiled to myself, thinking, soon Bourbon would be sleeping with the fish.

The following morning I spoke with the Squad 5 member who was the security guard at Ladder 18. He said, when Captain Bourbon climbed in bed with the fish there was a horrific scream, "what the fuck, who the fuck did this!, mother fucker................. mother fucker."

The security guard said he was questioned by Bourbon on how this could happen. He said he told Bourbon that he was sound asleep in the kitchen on the cot and heard nothing. He also said that he was on medication to help him sleep. Strict orders from the Fire Dept. medical office.

Bourbon simply had no clue how this was at all possible???

I never heard another word about the incident. It is my belief, the Captain was so embarrassed and did not want the story to get out.

At the Squad our lips were sealed.

To this day, whenever I happen to see a fish lying dead on a beach or street I think of Captain Bourbon in bed with that maggot infested fish! It brings a smile to my lips. It could not have happened to a better man.

30

THE JUNGLE

Summer 1980

During a softball season it was not unusual to play ball on more than one team. For two years I pitched for a team in Kearny, New Jersey, called The Jungle, which was a local bar that sponsored the team. After playing our games, which were mostly at night, we players would go to the bar for a few beers.

My wife Barbara asked for the first time in over two years, "What is this Jungle team?" I told her it was sponsored by a pet shop in Kearny.

One night Barbara decides to come and watch The Jungle play a game. There was a crowd of about 250 local fans in the stands, along with Barbara, watching the game.

I am on the pitching mound in the middle of the game, around the 5th inning, I hear this loud, ultrahigh pitched voice, call from Barbara, "Paul", "Paul", "Paul."

Everyone got real quiet. I tried to focus my eyes from the mound as to where Barbara was sitting in the stands. The high, bright lights were making it difficult.

I finally saw her as she was standing waving her hands and I called back, "What, What?"

She answered back at me, "It's The Jungle, The Jungle, it's not a pet shop, it's a GO, GO bar."

I waited for a moment then responded, "Really?????"

The laughter from the crowd was deafening.

Every local in the stands there knew The Jungle. I got away with the pet shop story for two years, and every time I meet with old friends from Kearny, we laugh about it. It was a great place to go after a game for a few beers.

31

SIX 10-92'S IN BROOKLYN GHETTO

1970

During the summer of 1970, I was the officer working a night tour (6PM-9AM) covering a vacation spot in Engine Company 290, located at 480 Sheffield Avenue, East New York section of Brooklyn, the busiest fire company in New York City, deep in the heart of the Ghetto. Also quartered with E-290 was Ladder Company 103 and Ladder Company 103-2.

The East New York area started suffering from urban blight during the 1950's and 1960's. Urban renewal laid waste to this area. The middle class moved out and the poor people moved into the area. Buildings started to deteriorate and the fire-load skyrocketed. It appeared that East New York was burning at all hours of the day and night. False alarms also skyrocketed. Between 60 to 65 percent of fire alarms were false. Fire companies in this area were responding to over ten thousand alarms a year.

At the start of my tour, approximately 6:30 PM, Engine Company 290 and I responded to a fire alarm located close to the firehouse. Due to the many years that had past, my memory has failed as to the exact location. Once, we arrived, after checking the area, I transmitted a 10-92, a code for a malicious false alarm.

We returned to quarters. Within 10 minutes the same fire alarm box was transmitted. Off we go, checking the area. Again, I transmitted a 10-92. This occurred three more times, in intervals of about 20 minutes. Each time I transmitted a 10-92. Five false alarms at the same box in a little over an hour!!!

Back at quarters, twenty minutes passed, and again we responded to the same location. Looking for fire and seeing none, I transmitted the 10-92.

Immediately after transmitting the 10-92, a young child came yelling, "Bombero, Bombero, there is a fire", pointing to a building down the block. We rolled up to the front of the four story building he was pointing to, and went inside. On the second floor there was a small, cushioned chair smoldering on fire.

Ladder Co. 103 removed the chair from the building and placed it next to a nearby fire hydrant. We opened the hydrant and put out the fire by soaking it with water. It was always a practice to remove something like this from a building, whether it was a smoldering chair or mattress. This was done to prevent rekindling.

We took up from the fire scene and returned to quarters. However, I never changed the 10-92 to a fire.

A half hour later, the same alarm box transmitted. We responded, and upon arrival I looked down the block to the building where we removed the chair. Fire was blowing out all the windows on the second and third floors.

A woman in the street was yelling, "Ah don't know how the first fi-a started. But, the second fi-a started because the fi-amans never put out the first fi-a."

We stretched a hand line into the building, knocking down all fire on the second floor. Another engine company stretched a line and knocked down all visible fire on the third floor.

The Battalion chief at the scene didn't know what the hell was going on, wondering what the woman was yelling about.

When I transmitted the 10-92 earlier, all the other companies responding, including the chief, turned around and never got to the scene.

The chief saw the chair by the fire hydrant and started asking questions. He came to me. I told him the truth. That I just left it as a false alarm because it was only a smoldering chair. He understood and said he would take care of it.

On a sidewalk nearby was a new looking refrigerator, a TV and some chairs and a table. I wish I saw this earlier. It was an obvious clue that the tenants were ready to burn themselves out, looking to get relocated to new housing. There by keeping some of their furniture. This was the norm for this area.

Many times responding to alarms, we noticed a U-Haul trailer parked in front of a building. We knew it wouldn't be long before an apartment, in that building, would be ablaze. The tenant getting new housing as a result. If a tenant was burned out, they were immediately placed to the top of a waiting list for new housing. I won't go there how the new housing looked one year later!

32

HELL'S HUNDRED ACRES

July 12, 1962

In 1960 when I was transferred from Ladder Company 10 to Rescue Company 1, FDNY, Manhattan, New York, Firefighter John Farragher was the first one to welcome and introduce me to my fellow firefighters. Immediately, he took me under his wing making sure that I was comfortable in my new surroundings, which included taking time to show me all the equipment on the rescue rig. It wasn't long before we became the closest of friends.

During the summer of 1962, NBC's DuPont Show of The Week, produced a documentary about Rescue Company 1. It was titled "Fire Rescue" and narrated by actor Walter Matthau. Matthau was best known for his role as Oscar Madison in the Odd Couple. For three months NBC and their camera crew filmed Rescue Company 1, both at the firehouse and on the road.

On the evening of July 12, 1962, Rescue Company 1 responded to Manhattan fire alarm Box 164. Because of the loss of firefighter lives, this area was known as "Hell's Hundred Acres."

A four alarm fire swept through a five story loft building at 390 Broadway, killing Farragher.

ALWAYS WANTED TO BE FIREMAN

Dream Lies in Ashes

By STEPHEN PELLETIERE

It's smybolic, in a tragic way, that the boyhood dream of John Farragher should today lie in ashes.

For it was in ashes that they found the body of John Farragher yesterday.

"John dreamed of being a fireman from the time he was a little boy," his widow, Mrs. Catherine Farragher, told a Journal-American reporter.

DISCUSSED DANGER

"Did he ever contemplate the danger?"

"Oh, we discussed it." She said in a tone that plainly precluded further probing, as though the intimate conversations a man has with his wife — especially about death and danger—are part of his legacy to her and not to be shared with strangers.

At 8:30 p.m. Thursday Fireman Farragher and his mates of Rescue Co. 1 responded to a blaze at 390 Broadway, in the area firemen have labeled—in the light-hearted way of men who face danger and kid about it—"Hell's 100 Acres."

Fireman Farragher followed his chief, Capt. John Rooney, into the blazing building. A blast of flame and fumes drove them back. It was not until Capt. Rooney was on the street that he noticed Mr. Farragher was missing.

His body was recovered yesterday, pinned beneath a grotesque fabrication of blackened, twisted steel.

And now a reporter is asking Mrs. Farragher: "What do you do now?"

Her answer is a sigh.

"What does anyone do?"

The reporter recalls Fireman Farragher was decorated for bravery in the U.S.S. Constellation fire. Was it only one citation he had, or were there others?

"I have a letter somewhere," the widow says. **"There were 13—or maybe 18—people he saved.**

"Someone once checked the records and found he had six citations. I don't know. He didn't know, either."

This, then, is Fireman Farragher's legacy to his city.

Thirteen — or maybe 18 — people alive who wouldn't be, were it not for him.

And his legacy to his four adopted children is — six pieces of paper, attesting to their father's heroism.

During fire operations, it was reported Farragher was missing on one of the upper floors. The following morning, Friday the 13th, Farragher was recovered buried beneath burnt roofing debris on the top floor.

It is Fire Department protocol that removal of the fallen will be done by the members of his company. In this case it was, Rescue Company 1. The photo below shows members of Rescue Company 1 gently placing Farragher in a waiting ambulance. The third person in the lower left corner with the number 1 shown on the helmet's front piece is me.

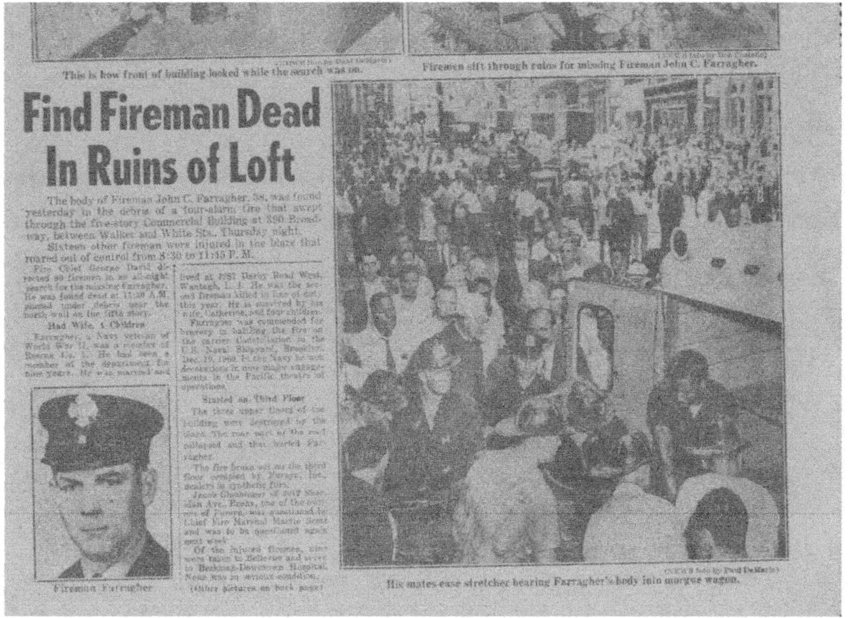

This is how front of building looked while the search was on.

Firemen sift through ruins for missing Fireman John C. Farragher.

Find Fireman Dead In Ruins of Loft

The body of Fireman John C. Farragher, [illegible], was found yesterday in the debris of a four-alarm fire that swept through the five-story Commercial Building at 890 Broadway, between Walker and White Sts., Thursday night.

Sixteen other firemen were injured in the blaze that roared out of control from 8:30 to 11:45 P. M.

Fire Chief George David directed 80 firemen in an all-night search for the missing Farragher. He was found dead at 11:[illegible] A.M. pinned under debris near the north wall on the fifth story.

Had Wife, 4 Children

Farragher, a Navy veteran of World War II, was a member of Rescue Co. 1. He had been a member of the department for [illegible] years. He was married and lived at [illegible] Road West, Wantagh, L. I. He was the second fireman killed in line of duty this year. He is survived by his wife, Catherine, and four children.

Farragher was commended for bravery in battling the fire on the carrier Constellation in the U.S. Navy Shipyard, Brooklyn, Dec. 19, 1960. In the Navy he won decorations in nine major engagements in the Pacific theatre of operations.

Started on Third Floor

The three upper floors of the building were destroyed by the blaze. The rear part of the roof collapsed and that buried Farragher.

The fire broke out on the third floor occupied by [illegible], Inc., dealers in synthetic furs.

[illegible] of [illegible] Sheridan Ave., Bronx, one of the owners of [illegible], was questioned by Chief Fire Marshal [illegible] and was to be questioned again next week.

Of the injured firemen, nine were taken to Bellevue and seven to Beekman-Downtown Hospital. None was in serious condition.

(Other pictures on back page)

Fireman Farragher

His mates ease stretcher bearing Farragher's body into morgue wagon.

NBC's DuPont Show of the Week featured in their documentary, "Fire Rescue" which showed the recovery of Farragher.

John was a World War II Navy veteran who won decorations in nine major engagements in the Pacific theatre of operations. He was married and lived in Wantagh, Long Island, New York and was survived by his wife Catherine and four children.

Soon after John was put to rest, members of Engine Company 65 and Rescue Company 1 decided to get together at John's house. There were sixty of us off duty. We spent three days working at his house doing repairs such as plumbing, roof repairs, painting, grass cutting, and electrical work. Catherine, John's wife kept us fed during the day. We gave small jobs for the kids to do giving them a chance to feel close to us. We shared stories with John's kids about how great a firefighter their dad was.

My job was to paint the exterior of his home. Once our work was completed, we all reveled with pride and contentment in what we had done to honor the memory of John and help his family.

33

RAIL RECCE OVER NORTH KOREA

February 1953

In my younger years I always wanted to join the Fire Department New York and become a firefighter.

However, here is a combat story of a different matter.

It is about 300 hours (3AM) on Feb 3rd, 1953, the weather is clear, there is a full moon, and it's bitter cold; 20 to 30 degrees below zero. Our crew is wearing heated suits, praying that they continue to keep us warm.

We are somewhere east over enemy North Korea. The B-26 Invader's engines are purring like kittens and powering us just over the snow covered mountain peaks of North Korea. It reminded me of the Frozen Chosen. I now knew what the Marines meant about the cold!

We were on a rail reconnaissance mission looking for trains headed south carrying supply's to the front lines at the 38th parallel.

The pilot gently took our B-26 down into a valley. Railroad tracks were clearly visible due to the refection of the full moon. We were flying about 75 to 150 feet above the terrain. Our indicated air speed was about 220 miles per hour. It was almost like day light, the moon and snow made it so clear. Trees were covered with snow.

As we continued following the tracks north, I imagined what was going through both the pilot and navigator's minds, "please no cables, please." The North Koreans were known for stretching cables across the valleys from one mountain peak to another. This was done hoping to snag a propeller or some part of the aircraft, trying bring it down. None of our crew wanted to be guests of the North Koreans.

I scanned through my gun sights looking for a train. The gun sight was similar to the periscope on a submarine, only it had an upper and lower sight that changed in mid-range to the upper or lower turrets. If there was a train out there it wasn't going to get away.

Suddenly, from both sides of the aircraft, golf balls of fire came down at us from the mountain tops. A major difference was these were deadly and much closer together, coming straight at us from both sides, trailing fire. Here we are flying in an aircraft and anti-aircraft fire (triple AAA) is coming down at us.

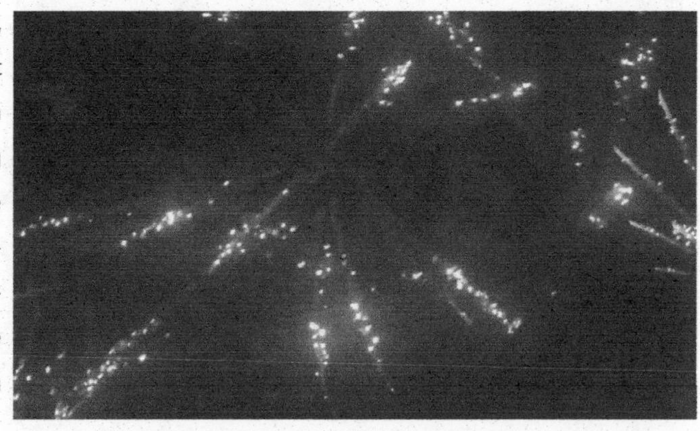

The North Koreans opened fire from all directions with automatic weapons. Tracers (bullets with fire trailing them) started to come up at us from the front as well as directly below. I had heard about being "hosed" (a term combat crews use when flying into this type of hornets nest) from other crews and now know firsthand what it feels like.

I wanted to radio to the pilot to "brake left" or "brake right" however, impossible with mountains on either side. The flack was so beautiful in color, but very, very terrifying, deadly and intense. Fortunately, I did not stain my pants and returned fire with both my twin 50 cal. machine guns at targets visible. This was a real Ground to Air and Air to Ground fire fight. I was praying I would not burn out my barrels because I was giving them all I had.

Thank God they never found their mark, as we passed thought it safely. Suddenly, it became quiet as we continued north. It was one of the most terrifying times of my life. Sixty seconds of pure hell into a real live hornet's nest.

Things were quiet and we continued following the railroad tracks north. The pilot brought us to a higher altitude, around 500 feet for a better view. The navigator/bombardier spotted steam coming from the stack of a locomotive headed south pulling about twelve railroad cars. The pilot immediately climbed to a more favorable altitude for a safe bomb drop. A 500 lb. bomb could cause damage to our aircraft if we got too close to the ground and blast.

In an instant, while we returned for the bomb run, the locomotive was disconnected and the railroad cars were separated in to clusters of four. The locomotive disappeared into a tunnel. We never were able to figure that one out. My guess there was a rail switch nearby and tracks led to the tunnel.

On the bomb run the bombardier radioed the information for lining up the aircraft on the target, then released four 500 lb. wing mounted bombs. A direct hit destroyed all four railroad cars and cut the railroad tracks.

After making wide a wide search we located a tunnel. We made three bomb runs on the entrance to the tunnel in an attempt to seal the locomotive in, dropping the remaining six 500 lb. bombs from the bomb bay. There appeared to be no exit from the tunnel. The one end we successfully sealed.

We returned making repeated strafing attacks at about 150 ft. above the terrain on the remaining railroad cars. Each time we pulled off the target I released a barrage of 50 caliber armor piercing incendiary (API) bullets from my turrets into all visible railroad cars setting them on fire.

We left the scene after all our ordinances was exhausted. Many of the railroad cars were in flames. Flashes of small arms being fired at us could be seen, hopefully, with no hits.

After returning back to K 9 AFB, Pusan, South Korea we checked our B-26 for any flak damage. Not one hole. How lucky can you get?

We went to the debriefing shack reporting the results and location of our attack. Also reporting the location of the "hornets' nest". The next, combat crews going north will avoid that area.

34

DENVER, COLORADO

June 1952

My first visit to jail while serving in the United States Air Force, July, 1952

In June of 1951, I graduated from Tottenville High School, Staten Island, New York and shortly afterward, November 16, 1951, I enlisted in the United States Air Force. My basic training was at Samson Air Force Base, Geneva, New York. After basic training I was transferred to Lowry Air Force Base in Denver, Colorado.

I was assigned to a sixteen week training course titled, Turret System Mechanic. At that time I was not aware that this course was a prerequisite to gunnery school for the B-29 heavy bomber or the Douglas B-26 Invader, an attack bomber. I studied hard and received top marks. Two students who scored the highest grades in the class were assigned as gunners on the B-26. I was one of them.

During the sixteen week training period, there were many boring days. So, on that free time five of us airmen would take a car ride to interesting places around Denver. We toured different parks, the Rocky Mountains, etc.

One night while riding through the streets of Denver, one of the guys came up with an idea with a great way to kill our boredom. We all had to draw straws and the one who drew the shortest straw had to get into the trunk of the car. Once in the trunk, dangle his arm out while the others spread catsup on it. This was to make it appear that there was a dead body in the trunk! As luck have you, I drew the shortest straw.

Once I climbed inside the trunk, the lid was closed just enough allowing my arm to visibly hang. Once set up, we rode through the busy streets of Denver. In no time, screams were heard from pedestrians walking on the sidewalk! The screams continued as we turned onto each new street. We were having fun for about an hour.

Oh, Oh! While stopped at an intersection, I could see a motorcycle cop behind us through the small opening in the trunk. I had no idea how long he was there. Slowly, I started to bring my arm back into the trunk hoping he didn't see it. However, before I could get my arm all the way in, the cop accelerated towards the car on his motorcycle, kicking the trunk lid, hurting my arm!

The cop ordered us to pull over and for the driver to get out of the car. I then decided it was a good time to climb out of the trunk. Wrong!! The cop yelled, "Get back in that trunk!" "I'm not getting back into the trunk", I yelled back!

"OK, you are all getting arrested."

"OK, I'll get back into the trunk." I said

"Too late!" He then radioed for the Patty Wagon to come and pick us up.

When the Patty Wagon arrived, the cop arrested me and the driver. Then off we headed to the slammer! Once there, we were booked for disorderly conduct and put into a cell.

An hour later the other three airmen arrived to bail us out. They waited just outside the police Captain's office, his door open, waiting to talk to him. They heard the Captain talking on the telephone.

"No, madam, it was not a body, simply some Lowry airmen pulling a prankster. We have it under control!" He hung up the phone and mumbled, "Over eighty calls!"

The three airmen after hearing the Captain, turned around and ran as quickly as possible out of the police station. There was no way in hell did they want to be guests of the Denver City Jail!!!

After one night in jail the Air Police came to bail us out and bring us back to the base. We both were given an Article 15 for punishment, kitchen duty. We had to peel potatoes, wash dishes and wash barrack windows.

Not too long after, I was transferred from this squadron to the Douglas B-26 gunnery school. All penalties remained behind with the other squadron. After B-26 gunnery school it was off to combat crew training at Langley Air Force Base, Virginia.

June 1956

ME!

THE POLICE BEAT

Swift Kick Rewards 'Catsuped' Prankster

By THE NEWS POLICE REPORTERS

Summer and pranksters seem to go hand in hand, but **Patrolman Earl Williamson** thinks he may have cured at least one Lowry airman of further foolishness.

Patrolman Williamson got onto this case when he spotted a car with an arm hanging out of the back trunk with what appeared to be blood splattered over both the arm and the trunk lid.

The officer stopped the car and assured himself that there was life in the body attached to the arm by not too gently kicking the trunk lid. The blood turned out to be catsup.

Just as effective as taking the pulse the officer surmised, and twice as good in teaching a lesson to boys with morbid senses of humor.

* * *

35

AIRLINE CRASH

December 16, 1960

On the morning of December 16, 1960 at 10:45 am, a TWA Lockheed Constellation airline and a United Airlines DC-8, collided in midair in a blinding snowstorm over New York City, raining death on the city.

DC-8 Jet Airliner

At the time of the accident it was considered the worst aviation disaster in the history of commercial flying. When it was over, one hundred and twenty eight people from both planes, plus six on the ground had lost their lives. After the collision the Constellation broke into three parts, hurling forty-four people to their death. The plane or what was left of it, crashed in the fields of the Miller Army Base, in Staten Island, New York.

The flaming wreckage of the DC 8 continued flying until crashing into the Pillar of Fire Church at the intersection of Sterling Place and 7th Avenue in the Park Slope section of Brooklyn. The crash ignited a seven-alarm blaze which claimed an undetermined amount of lives.

Rescue Company 1 is busy with committee work at the firehouse, located on West 43rd Street between 5th and 6th Avenues in Manhattan, New York. Over the New York Fire Department bell alarm system a third alarm was transmitted for alarm box located at the corner of Sterling Place and 7th Avenue, Brooklyn, New York. Immediately after the bell alarm sounded for the third alarm, the department phone in quarters rang. Rescue's officer Lieutenant Michael Jeris answered the phone and was ordered by the dispatcher to immediately respond to the third alarm in Brooklyn. No information was given on the fire, only to immediately respond. Everyone just boarded the rig and off we went. What no one knew, what was to unfold in the upcoming hours was to remain with us the rest of our lives.

Weather was cold and it was snowing lightly while responding. Not unusual for a December morning. Traffic was light and we were able to respond safely yet quickly. Besides the Rescue's driver there were five firefighters and one officer working that day. Unfortunately the radio on the Rescue rig malfunctioned. It took us about 20 minutes to arrive at the fire scene still not knowing any particulars of the fire.

We pulled on to Seventh Avenue and stopped about a half block from the alarm box location. I jumped off the rear step, went around to the side of the rig and saw to my horror, the huge tail section of the DC 8 jet airliner. It was sitting on a burning car at the intersection of Sterling Place and 7th Avenue. The large name United, clearly visible, painted on the side of the tail section.

Lt. Jeris received orders from the Chief in charge for the company to stretch a hand line into one of the burning tenements near the corner. We stretched a hand line from a nearby engine company to the fourth floor of the corner building. No sooner then we got water in the line it burst from the water pressure. Immediately, we radioed to the pumper operator and had the line shut down, then replaced the burst length of hose with another. Starting water again, all of us soaking wet, we then were able to advance on the burning fire. After knocking down all visible fire, looking down from a rear window could be seen what was left of the Pillar of Fire church.

Returning to the street we began searching through the wreckage of the aircraft. Lifting a large piece of the aluminum section of the fuselage off the seats revealed a sight I wish on no one. Two young women were still strapped tightly in their safety belts. The look of horror was expressed on their faces. They were clean and looked as if they just strapped themselves into their seats and went to sleep.

There was one survivor, 11 year old Stephen Baltz. The little boy lay in a hospital bed, burned and bloody, his leg broken. Working to save his life were a team of 18 doctors and 15 nurses. He had been on the United Airlines flight and was thrown clear into a snow bank. People nearby rushed to his aid putting out his flaming clothing. By his side the following day was his mother and father when he perished.

FINAL DAILY NEWS 5¢

AIR CRASH RAINS DEATH ON CITY

Amid Tragedy, a Small Miracle

The Air Disaster: 7 Full Pages of NEWS Staff Fotos

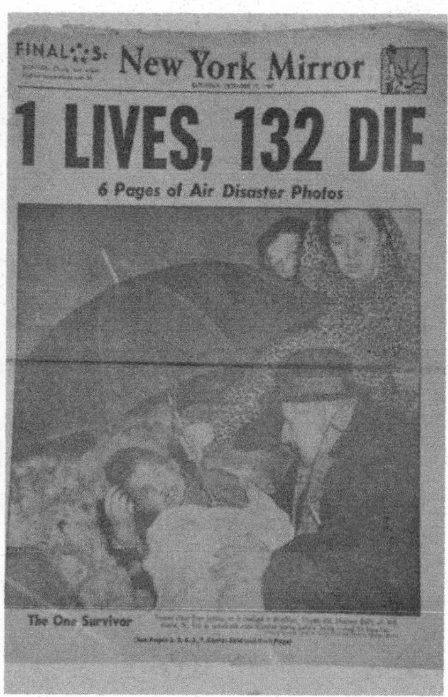

FINAL New York Mirror

1 LIVES, 132 DIE

6 Pages of Air Disaster Photos

The One Survivor

The rest of the day was searching local buildings for victims and placing bodies into the make shift morgue. We were soaking wet and cold. Around 7 PM we were relieved by Rescue Company's night shift who brought us needed dry clothing. What was to unfold three days later on Dec. 19, 1960 is another story. It never ends being a New York City firefighter.

36

USS CONSTELLATION

December 19, 1960

USS Constellation, a Kitty Hawk-class supercarrier, was the third ship of the United States Navy to be named in honor of the "new constellation of stars". The contract to build the Constellation was awarded to the New York Naval Shipyard, Brooklyn, New York, on July 1, 1956, and her keel was laid down 14 September 1957 at the New York Navy Yard. She was launched October 8, 1960. Nickname "Connie" and cost US$ 264.5 million.

The USS Constellation was heavily damaged by fire while under construction on December 19, 1960. The carrier was in the final stages of construction at the Brooklyn Navy Yard in Brooklyn when the fire began.

The fire broke out when a forklift operating on the hanger deck accidentally pushed its cargo into a steel plate knocking it over. The plate then broke off a plug of a 500 gallon tank of diesel fuel which spilled from the container reaching the lower levels of the ship. Fuel was ignited perhaps by a cutting torch of a fitter and then moved to wooden scaffolding. The flames spread quickly filling the passageways of the ship with smoke.

It took 17 hours for firefighters to extinguish the fire, some of whom had been driven to the raw edge of exhaustion after being at the Park Slope air accident. The firefighters saved hundreds of lives without losing any of their own.

Rescue Company 1 with its crew arrived shortly after the fire started. Upon arrival, Lieutenant William McMahon was ordered to make search below the hanger deck where to fire was raging.

Working in teams connected by lifelines, Lt. McMahon, Firefighter Thomas Bonamo and Firefighter Timothy Costello threaded their way through a maze of compartments and passageways. In their search, 22 workers were located and moved to safety.

The fire was battled for twelve hours. Fifty workers were killed and 385 were injured.

My shift was the night shift. When we arrived all rescues were completed by the day shift. Our orders were to make secondary searches below decks. During our search unfortunately we recovered four dead workers huddled together in a closed closet three decks below. I was hoping this late into the fire everyone was recovered.

I might add my shift had just returned to work after the Park Slope plane crash. Our turn out gear still wet with the smell of death on it.

37

CHINATOWN FIRE

1971

As a Lieutenant, I was assigned to Squad Company 5, FDNY, located in Chinatown, Manhattan, New York City.

It was a hot, summer afternoon, when a fire broke out in an apartment on the fourth floor of a six story tenement, located at 245 Eldridge St., Chinatown, in Manhattan, NY. Squad Co. 5 was assigned and responded.

Upon arrival, smoke and fire was pushing out from the fourth floor windows. The first due, an engine company, was already hooking up to a hydrant, while other members were stretching a hand line up the interior staircase.

People were crowded on the front fire escape, as well as coming out the front door, carrying suitcases. In Chinatown, residents were always seen carrying a suitcase when escaping a fire.

Firefighter, Jack Cafaro of Squad Company 5, and I entered the front of the building. Without the protection of the Scott Air Pack, we quickly climbed the interior staircase, bumping into many escaping tenants.

When we reached a fourth floor apartment, flames were rolling out from a hallway doorway! While in the hallway, we ducked below the flames, past the fire, and climbed the staircase to the fifth floor. (This being the most dangerous position, getting above the fire.) We did a quick search of the two fifth floor apartments and located no one. We continued our search to the sixth floor.

At that time, I was hoping the engine company, who were stretching their line, would do it quickly, so as to get water on the fire!

Cafaro and I were taking a heavy feed, as the stairway above was rapidly filling with smoke. (Feed in FDNY language means breathing in smoke)

We searched a top floor apartment, but didn't find anyone. In the second apartment, we located three people; a man, a woman and a small boy. The man was sitting on a window sill, holding the boy in his arms. He had tied telephone wire under his arm pits in an attempt to lower the boy six stories to the street below. This being a foolish idea because telephone wire is manufactured of an extremely thin gauge copper wire. No way could it support the weight of the boy!!

If I arrived a few seconds later, the man would have attempted to lower the boy, thus causing him to fall six stories to his death! I immediately untangled the wire and took the boy in my arms.

Firefighter Cafaro, carried the woman and headed back down the stairway, while I followed with the boy, the man closely behind me. We moved as quickly as possible.

Once we reached the fire floor, Cafaro and I placed our backs to the fire apartment, protecting the victims we were carrying in our arms. This allowing the man and woman to go past the fire which was spewing from the doorway. I followed closely behind shielding the little boy from the flames with my body.

FF Cafaro and I were able to get all three of the victims safely to the street. We were treated for smoke inhalation and minor burns at the scene.

This rescue was completed without Scott Air Pak's or the presence of an operating hand line.

Two Island firemen save 3 in blaze

Two Staten Island firemen rescued three persons, including a 7-year-old boy, from a burning tenement yesterday on Manhattan's Lower East Side.

Lt. Paul Geidel of 378 Sleight Ave., Tottenville, and Fireman John Cafaro, of 124 Fabian St. Port Richmond, assigned to Emergency Squad 5 in Chinatown, rescued Moncerata Ramos, 46, her son, Raymond, and Julia Marianas, 25. They were trapped in their apartments, and escape routes were cut off by the flames, fire officials said.

The two rescuers used their bodies as shields and carried them from the burning building.

Nine persons were assisted by firemen. Five were treated for smoke inhalation.

The fire in the six-story building originated shortly after 2:30 p.m. in a fourth floor apartment at 245 Eldridge St., and spread to the above floor.

38

EKLAND PENNSYLVANIA TOURNAMENT

September 1975

I was invited to pitch softball with a team from Middletown, New York, sponsored by a local bar named Players as well as the team name. We were invited to an AA Fast Pitch tournament in Elkland, Pennsylvania. A popular tournament around Labor Day each year. There were about forty teams enrolled in the tournament. The softball complex was made up of five beautiful manicured ball fields. At the main field the grandstands which were built in the early forties and made of wood were old, but beautifully built.

The night before the tournament it rained pretty hard and it was questionable if there would even be a tournament. However, the following morning the sun shined brightly. Not a cloud in the sky. We were scheduled to play a nine AM game.

My wife, Barbara and I arrived early at the complex parking area. The five softball fields were nearby and located next to one another.

We just walked out onto the fields looking for which one we were scheduled to play on. It was a clear, but damp morning, bleachers wet. We walked past a couple of dugouts where other teams were suiting up, getting ready for play.

While walking together, Barbara leaves me. She walked over to a dug out where about seventeen ball players were suiting up. She bends over, leans into the dugout and asks, "Does anyone have something in there that I can sit on?"

I couldn't believe what I just heard and kept on walking away. How can a beautiful woman ask a bunch of raunchy ball players if they have something she can sit on? She got plenty of replies, all respectful and many laughs. Once she caught up with me, I noticed her face was bright red!

39

I WAS LUCKY TO SURVIVE

Summertime in the Mid-Seventies

I was the officer working the night tour at Rescue Company 1, Manhattan, New York City. During this time period, Engine Company 65 shared their fire house with Rescue Company 1 on 43rd Street.

Once roll was called, jobs were assigned which included a roof man, an outside vent man, a force-able entry team, and a can man who also carried a six foot hook.

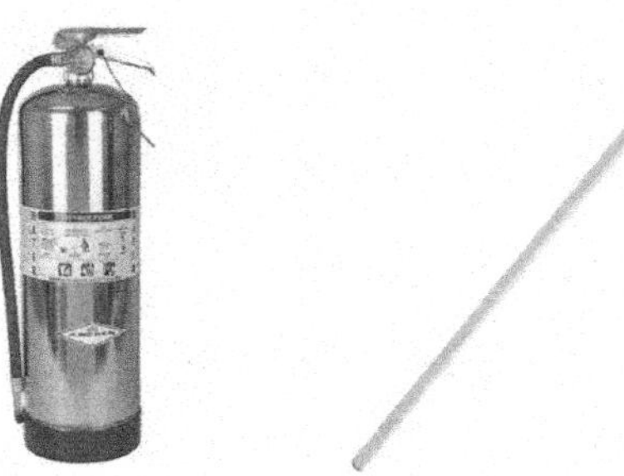

(The can is a 2 ½ gallon water pressurized fire extinguisher)

Time had blurred my memory as to which members of the Rescue Company 1 firefighters were working that night. However, I do remember three; Firefighter Ronald Foote, Firefighter James McCarthy and Firefighter Michael Maloney.

During this time period, Engine Company 65 shared their fire house with Rescue Company 1 on 43rd Street.

Immediately after roll call, a civilian entered our quarters reported a fire located on the third floor of a hotel only a few doors down from the firehouse. Both companies immediately responded.

Once at the fire building, we climbed the stairway to the third floor. The fire was burning through the door of one of the apartments, filling the hallway with extreme heat and thick black smoke. Further down the hallway, on the other side of this flaming door, we heard a woman screaming for help.

Immediately, Firefighter Foote approached the front of the burning door while he operated the fire extinguisher. He knocked down most of the fire on the burning door and also some in the apartment behind.

Firefighter Maloney immediately proceeded past Foote and the fire!! He grabbed the trapped woman at the same time staying very low, carrying her back down the hallway past the fire to safety.

Picture below is Firefighter Maloney being congratulated by woman he rescued.

In the meantime, Engine Company 65 had hooked up a 2 ½ inch hand line to the stand pipe on the floor below the fire, and stretched it to the third floor.

Once they got water, they advanced their line to the doorway knocking down all visible fire in the apartment. A quick search of the apartment found no one inside.

Firefighter Foote was transported by ambulance to Bellevue Hospital with burns of both hands.

Once the fire had been declared under control, Rescue 1 was ordered to take up.

We drove to the hospital to get Foote. Pulling onto the street in front of the hospital, our truck head lights reflected brightly off the yellow stripes on Foote's turnout coat. He was standing tall in the middle of the street. Both of his hands were bandaged to the wrist with white gauze which was already beginning to unravel as he was holding his six foot hook. We picked him up and returned to quarters.

Once back in quarters, Foote and I went to my office located on the third floor. Before going up, I invited members from Engine Company 65 to join us to critique the fire. However, the firefighters of Engine 65 were busy preparing the evening meal as it was their month to cook.

Once, in my office with Foote, I broke out a bottle of Jack Daniels and offered him a shot. He didn't refuse, he took the bottle, opened it and poured some of the whiskey over the bandages on both hands, then put the bottle up to his lips drinking more than a shot. Deep, unclear, growling words came out of his mouth. The gauze wrapped around his both hands took on a magenta color from the whisky.

We soon heard the dinner bell ring. Time to eat. I asked Foote if he was coming down for the meal. He simply growled, "No, I'll stay here with the bottle." I left him alone and went downstairs to the kitchen.

After the meal I returned to my office, but not before inviting Lieutenant Rega and Engine Company 65 members to my office so we all can discuss the events of the fire.

I went over to my typewriter to type out the fire, injury and meritorious act reports. Foote was relaxed sitting in one of the office chairs.

A short time later Maloney and McCarthy walked into the office along with two firefighters from Engine 65. We talked about the fire and discussed if it could have been handled any different.

Lieutenant Rega of Engine 65, entered the office and sat on the recliner.

Not a minute went by when Foote suddenly stood up and yelled, with a low, growling voice, "Get the fuck out of the Rescue office," pointing to members of Engine 65. "Not you two, (the two firefighters from E-65), YOU Rega." Lt. Rega was sitting relaxed in the recliner. "YOU, get the fuck out of the Rescue office Foote repeated.

In a split second, Foote lunged at Rega placing both his hands firmly around Rega's throat, chocking him. Rega was gasping for air, trying to remove Foote's grasp. As the two struggled, Foote's gauze bandages were dangling from his wrists to the floor. McCarthy and Maloney stepped in and immediately grabbed Foote's wrists and yanked his grip free from Rega's throat. Rega, fell back into the recliner gasping for air, at the same time rubbing his throat and shaking his head.

Foote stepped back holding both his hands high, the gauze unraveled enough to show huge blisters on both of his ands.

I figured the shit was going to hit the fan. The case of a Rescue One firefighter strangling the officer of Engine 65. How can anyone explain what happened? You can't make this stuff up.

Lt. Rega stood up rubbing his throat, looked me straight in the eyes and simply said, "Paul, don't you ever invite me to your office again." Then he walked out shutting the door behind him. I never heard anything more about it. Thank God. This could have been a disaster.

Once he left, I asked Foote why he attacked Lt. Rega?

He simply replied, "I never liked that man."

I couldn't believe his reply. How stupid is that? I turned and went back to my typewriter to complete my reports.

Foote was placed on medical leave, went to the bunk room and fell asleep.

Another night in Rescue 1 that I will never forget.

Pictured below, left is Firefighter Ronald Spencer T. Foote and on the right is myself.

40

BELLEVUE

1960

Before my transfer to Rescue Company1, I spent three years with Ladder Company 10 where my firefighting experiences were limited because of the rarity of fire duty at this location. Once I reported for duty at Rescue Co. 1, I kept my mouth shut and concentrated on learning and remembering everything possible from the experienced firefighters of my new company.

On my first day, we were sent to the Bellevue Hospital morgue, which was located in the sub-basement of the hospital. The night before Rescue had a job where two people were killed. The victims were placed in two of Rescues body bags and removed to the morgue at Bellevue.

Once at the hospital, we took the elevator, which was a big, square metal cage, its top and four sides were also made of steel wire mesh, spaced far enough apart so one could see through it readily in all directions. The floor was made of diamond plate steel. To operate this antique, a brass handle had to be pushed to one side for up and the other side for down.

The elevator rattled and squeaked as it descended downward in the open shaft. It had to be the slowest moving elevator in the world. Several thick, black greasy

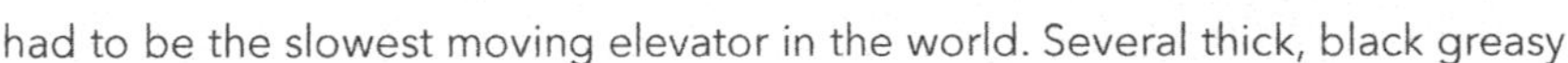

cables were seen through the side of the elevator as we were slowly moving down. Through the top of the elevator you could see these cables extend upward to the top of the shaft. They were wrapped around huge turning wheels. They were secured to hefty steel brackets attached to the top of the elevator. Finally, with a loud banging noise we stopped at the cement bottom of the elevator shaft.

Once there, we slid open the metal gate. There was a leather strap connected to the gate which had to be in an upright position to get out of the elevator.

The basement was poorly lit, the walls were wet and very damp with moisture. We saw an attendant standing by a metal door which had a small window located in the middle allowing light from inside. My Lieutenant went to the man and explained why we were there. After a brief conversation the two of them walked off to retrieve the body bags. The rest of us just waited patiently in the dark corridor milling around.

I walked over to the door and peeked through the small window. The room on the other side was huge. Ceiling lights hung above lighting the entire room. There were four stainless steel tables lined next to one another. On two of the tables were naked bodies with two men dressed in white robes hovering over the bodies. Realization set in as the hair on my arms stood up. I was viewing the morgue autopsy room.

A short time later, the officer returned with the attendant carrying two body bags. He handed them to us. We were about to leave when the attendant insisted we stay. He said he had something he wanted to show us. Then he ran down the dimly lit corridor. The sound of his heels echoing off the damp walls fading in the distance.

At that point, we all felt the same thing, let's get the fuck out of here! We waited a few seconds then all got in the elevator caring less about what he wanted to show us. I immediately pushed the brass lever to the up position. It seemed like forever for the circuit to cut in.

Suddenly from a distance we could hear the attendant yelling, "Wait a minute, wait a minute!!" His calls vibrating off the walls as he was running towards us from down the hallway. Again, the sound of heels echoing off the damp walls, only this time the sound was getting louder as he got closer and closer.

Finally at a snail's pace the elevator slowly began to rise off the basement floor. Through the scissor gate you could see the attendant running towards us. He was yelling again, "I have something I want to show you!" He was holding what appeared to be a large ball attached to strings.

It was too dark for us to see what it was. He realized we were not waiting for him. The elevator was moving extremely slow. We were only about three feet above the basement floor.

Suddenly, while on the run, and with the form of a professional bowler, he released this thing with perfect follow through. Rolling it as if it were a bowling ball down an alley. It bounced erratically, tumbling across the top of the damp concrete floor towards the elevator. The attached strings were flying wildly in all directions. At the same time the attendant cupping his hands around his mouth was screaming up to us, "we had this for seven years and don't know who it belongs to!" The bowling ball struck the bottom of the elevator shaft just below us with a muffled thud that rattled the gate. It bounced back after hitting the gate far enough for us to look down clearly and see what it was.

The bowling ball was a human head, the strings were long black hair!! The face was sickly gray, with the hair resting across the face. It laid there face up, eyes closed as if it were saying, "Hi."

The attendant below was laughing uncontrollably. He was bent over, his hands clasping his knees. His laugher, ghoulish. Turning his head slowly, he glanced upward as he raised his right hand gently waving goodbye. The elevator slowly took us up and out of sight. We had made his day.

41

HELLO AGAIN

1953-2017

Years after being discharged from the United States Air Force, history began back into my life. I read an article about the Air Force Museum at Wright Patterson Air Force Base in Dayton, Ohio and decided to visit one day.

I drove out to the museum from New York. What a beautiful museum it is. To see all the museum had to offer takes a few days. What I didn't expect was in the Korean War section. There was a Douglas B-26 C Invader from K-9 Air Force Base, Pusan, Korea. The B-26 from the 34th Bomb Squadron, 17th Bomb Group named "Dream Girl". I was shocked at first. I had flown two combat missions on this aircraft. I was assigned to the 95th Bomb Squadron but because I was a gunner without an assigned crew, I flew with other squadrons to complete my combat tour of combat missions.

Pictured below is myself peering through the Plexiglas nose of "Dream Girl" at K-9 Air Force Base, Pusan, Korea.

Also, me standing next to "Dream Girl" in one photo and second photo with fellow gunner Richard Schnipple at Wright Patterson Air Force Base, Dayton, Ohio.

After this experience I decided to do some homework on other B-26's from K-9, if they were anywhere in the USA.

I checked on "My Mary Lou" pictured below. "My Marie Lou" was assigned to the 95th Bomb Squadron at K-9 AFB, Pusan, Korea.

This picture is of my brother Richard giving "My Mary Lou" a boost on the butt.

My research discovered the following;

On June 27, 1993, at 1240 hours, central daylight time, a Douglas B26B, N8036E, collided with the ground in a field adjacent to a taxiway at the Greater Kankakee Airport, Kankakee, Illinois, during takeoff on runway 4. The Airline Transport Pilot and a single passenger received minor injuries. The aircraft was substantially damaged. The aircraft was departing from an on-going air show when the accident occurred. The pilot stated that at approximately 140 MPH he performed liftoff and immediately began losing substantial power on the right engine. The aircraft banked to the right and the right wingtip impacted the ground between the runway and taxiway.

Next on my list was the B-26 named "Monie" of the 37th Bomb

Squadron.

I was unable to find "Monie's" new home but Google found this picture of the aircraft and its crew. 1st Lt. Robert Mikesh was the pilot of this crew and later became the curator of United States Space Museum in Washington, DC.

Next on my search was "Sweet Miss Lillian." Below are photos of B-26 "Sweet Miss Lillian" warming up her twin R-2800 Pratt Whitney engines at K-9 Air Force Base, Pusan, Korea. Also a photo of the nose art.

While traveling in my motorhome in Riverside, California on Interstate 215, I noticed a sign for the March Air Force Base Museum, I decided to visit.

The first aircraft I saw while walking through the parking lot was "Sweet Miss Lillian. I was in shock, knock me over with a feather. After all these years there she is again, sitting as proud as ever. In the photos below time has taken its toll on us both.

Pictured are Nose Art of B-26's at K-9. I was unable to locate their final home but wanted to share them with you.

587
Lady Nan

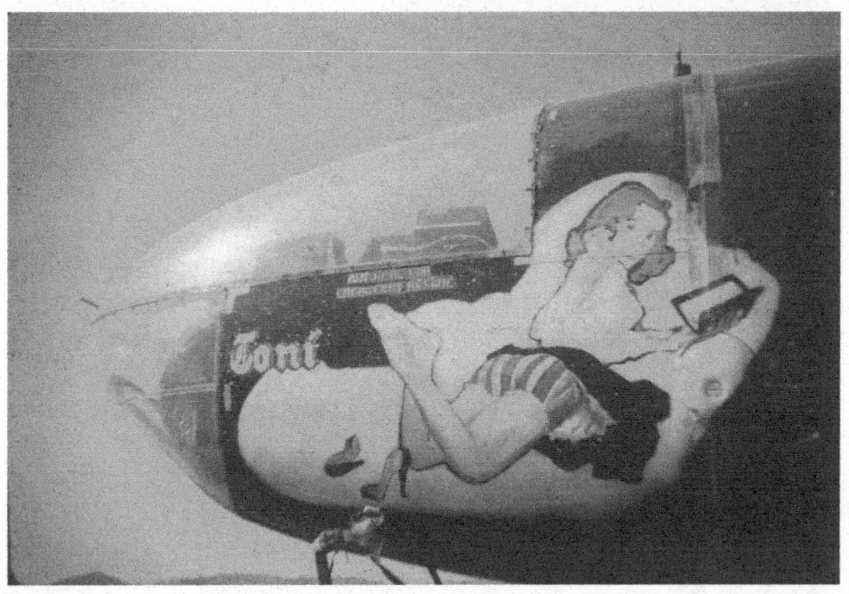
Toni

42

JOEY

1961

There always was a friend on the Fire Department that made you laugh whenever you were together. Joey was one of them. Joey and I both lived on Staten Island, New York. We traveled to work via the Staten Island Rapid Transit train to the last stop of the line, the Staten Island Ferry. The commute from my home in Tottenville was two hours and fifteen minutes each way. Tottenville is located in the most southern part of New York City. Joey was assigned to Engine Company 65, located at 43rd Street, Manhattan, New York. Engine Company 65 shared their firehouse with my company, Rescue Company 1.

Once on the ferry, we had a twenty-five minute ride to Manhattan, then a subway ride to mid-town Manhattan, followed by a brief fifteen minute walk to our firehouse.

On many occasions while riding to work together, soft mumbling sounds came from Joey's mouth. One time he mimicked a car crash. I looked around and noticed a vacant lot with a smashed up car from an accident. Other times he would mimic a bugle softly playing the taps, and I would quickly look around and see the American flag being lowered or raised. These soft mumbles went on for years, each time playing to whatever Joey was seeing at the time.

On the way home, as the ferry approached the dock on Staten Island, the passengers would crowd the front of the ferry. The rush was on to make their connection with a bus or the train. The train had to stay on schedule, so if the ferry was late getting in, the train would have to leave without the ferry passengers.

There were about eight telephone booths just outside the train station. If the train was still at the station, as many as ten or more people lined up at each telephone booth waiting to make their phone call home, to let their kin know which train they were catching in order to be picked up.

Joey devised a plan on how to get to the phone without waiting in the long line. As loud as he could while standing near the train, he would shout out, **"BOARD, ALL ABOARD, BOARD, ALL ABOARD."** And just like that, everyone ran to catch the train. No more waiting to make a phone call. Joey did this for years and got away with it!! He never had to wait to make a call!!

Every other month it was the responsibility of one of the two fire companies to go out and get the day or night tour meal. While working a night tour together, it was Joey's turn to get the meal for both companies. I was chosen to accompany Joey and help carry the meal back to the firehouse.

It was decided to purchase the meal at a local Chinese restaurant which was located in the Engine's administrative district. Joey wrote down the meal order from each one of the members of both companies, and off we went to get the meal. I might add that each member always doubled their order because this restaurant was known for skimping on the amount of food it provided to the customer.

I didn't know where we were going, so I just followed along with Joey. As I recall, it was somewhere around 49th Street. We walked towards this Chinese restaurant and saw an Asian man standing in front. Joey recognized the man and yelled "hello". The man looked, recognizing Joey, he clutched both hands in his face and ran back into the restaurant. I looked at Joey and asked, "What's this all about?" Joey didn't reply.

We walked inside the restaurant and in the lobby we saw the man again, who also happened to be the restaurant manager. Joey once again said hello to him, at the same time handing him the meal order list. With a firm voice Joey said, "Here is the firehouse meal order, we will be back in a short time to pick it up." Joey, patting him on the back. We left to a nearby café and got a soda while waiting.

15 minutes later we returned to the restaurant to pick up the order. The same man, the manager, came out with two huge bags filled with our order. Joey thanked him very much, they both shook hands, and Joey handed him five dollars. I never question the five dollar deal, I simply carried one of the filled bags back to the firehouse. I knew in some fire companies' administrative districts, restaurants loved the firefighters and fed them every so often as a courtesy. I guess thie was one of them.

Once back in the firehouse we sat down together enjoying every bit of our double-ordered meal.

After dinner things got quiet, and soon Joey was mumbling again, "woof, woof". I looked up at the TV mounted on the wall showing two puppies. Why wasn't I surprised??

43

AT&T FIRE

February 25, 1975

I was the officer working the night tour (6PM to 9AM) with Rescue Company I, on February 27, 1975. A 10-75, an all hands, was transmitted from Box 465 at approximately 12:30 AM, to 204 Second Avenue between 13th and 14th Streets. (An all hands in FDNY talk means all the companies that responded to an alarm box are put to work.)

Upon arrival we entered the first floor which was filled with thick smoke. We met, on that floor, a firefighter from Ladder Company 3. I asked him, "Why aren't

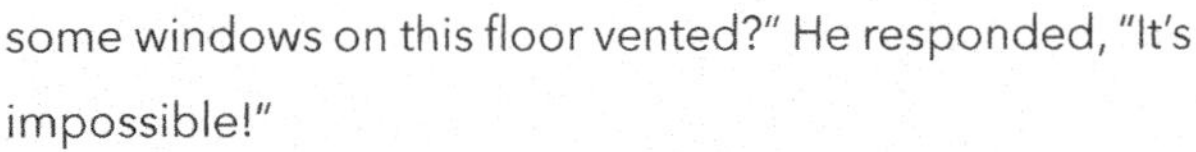

some windows on this floor vented?" He responded, "It's impossible!"

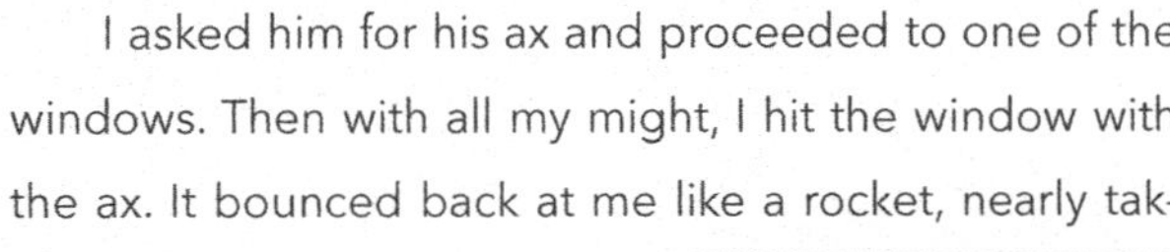

I asked him for his ax and proceeded to one of the windows. Then with all my might, I hit the window with the ax. It bounced back at me like a rocket, nearly taking off my head. The window was not glass, it was Lexan or Polycarbonate, a bullet-proof glass which for security reasons were put on the buildings lower two floor windows.

Rescue Company I and I proceeded to the 14th. Street side of the building in an attempt to vent the windows from the outside. The outer window frames were covered with metal mash shutters.

After we forced the shutters open, we discovered that the windows behind were made with wired glass and metal mullions. Breaking the wired glass was extremely difficult because we could only make small holes. Breaking the metal mullions was virtually impossible. However, we succeeded and were able to break through only to find Lexan as the final obstacle. Using our K-12 Partner Saw with a carbide blade, allowed us to cut through the Lexan like butter. Finally we were able to start venting the building. Heavy black smoke forced its way through the holes.

After we vented a couple of the windows, we proceeded back inside the building trying to locate the fire. We found the staircase to the basement and sub-basement. We tied a lifeline of rope to the lead man because the stairway was filled with thick foul-smelling black smoke and it was a precaution to keep us from being separated or lost. We were all wearing Scott Air Packs.

Following us, Engine Company 5 stretched a hand-line down the staircase.

At the bottom of the staircase in the sub-basement there was a door. The plastic escutcheons on the wall were melting. We knew the seat of the fire was just on the other side of that door. The captain of Engine Company 5 radioed to his motor pump operator to charge their line. Once water was in the line and fully charged, we forced the door open.

At a point in time, the warning bells on the Scotts of Engine 5 went off warning them there was little air remaining in their tanks. They had to leave their line. If they stayed, it was likely they would have never gotten out of the building alive. Engine companies never want to abandon their hand-lines. However, in this case, they had no choice. Death surely would have followed!

After we forced the door open, I saw the most beautiful colored fire I have ever encountered. The fire had complete control of what was later described as the cable vault. The cable vault was 18-by-22-by-300-foot. The fire was all the colors of the rainbow plus more!!

We opened the nozzle to get water on the fire. After operating the hand-line for a period of time, we advanced it into the room and knocked down the fire!

Immediately, I radioed to Division I, "Rescue Company I has knocked down all visible fire and it appears that it is under control." I wanted Rescue I to get the credit for locating and knocking down this fire.

WRONG! WRONG! I didn't know there were overhead ducks running upward throughout the building. That was a huge mistake on my part, since the fire burned another seventeen hours before it was brought under control. Thankfully, people were kind and did not bust my balls!!!

From the start to finish of this fire, I used twelve or more Scott Air Bottles, the most I had ever used at one fire during my firefighting career.

About ten in the morning, we were relieved by the day tour of Rescue I. They worked approximately another 7 hours. However, at the scene, every one of us that worked this fire, were treated for smoke inhalation and heat exhaustion. One rescue firefighter required sutures to his knee. Some were placed on medical leave. Smoke and fumes felled over 150 firefighters including 67 spectators who were in the vicinity.

Pictured here is the fire burning out of control at the time we were relieved 12 hours after I opened my big mouth. I wish I had never said that we put the fire under control. When the fire was finally placed under control, five alarms had been transmitted.

Pictured is the original medical report I submitted on March 7th, 1975.

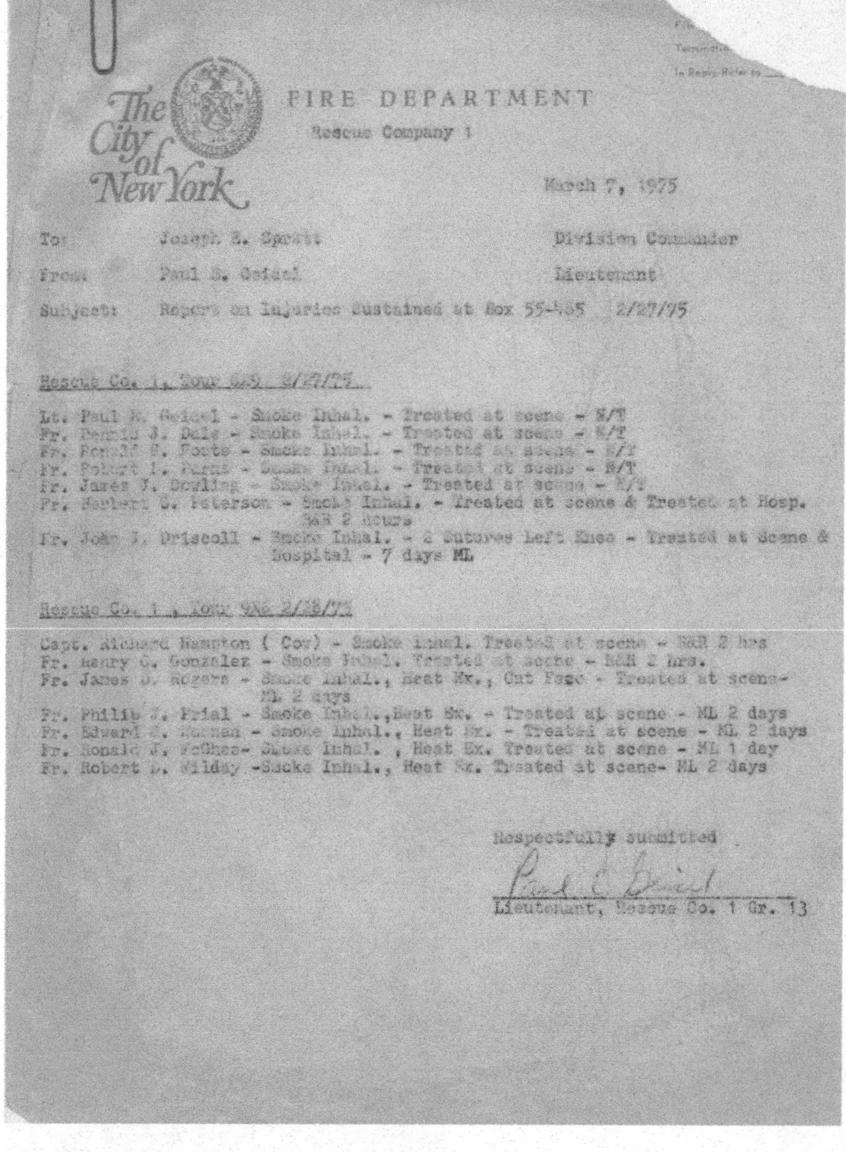

The City of New York

FIRE DEPARTMENT
Rescue Company 1

March 7, 1975

To: Joseph E. Spratt — Division Commander
From: Paul H. Geidel — Lieutenant
Subject: Report on Injuries Sustained at Box 55-465 2/27/75

Rescue Co. 1, Tour [illegible] 2/27/75

Lt. Paul H. Geidel - Smoke Inhal. - Treated at scene - N/T
Fr. Dennis J. Dale - Smoke Inhal. - Treated at scene - N/T
Fr. [illegible] Foote - Smoke Inhal. - Treated at scene - N/T
Fr. Robert [illegible] - Smoke Inhal. - Treated at scene - N/T
Fr. James J. Dowling - Smoke Inhal. - Treated at scene - N/T
Fr. Herbert C. Peterson - Smoke Inhal. - Treated at scene & Treated at Hosp. R&R 2 hours
Fr. John J. Driscoll - Smoke Inhal. - 2 Sutures Left Knee - Treated at Scene & Hospital - 7 days ML

Rescue Co. 1, Tour 9x6 2/28/75

Capt. Richard Hampton (Cov) - Smoke Inhal. Treated at scene - R&R 2 hrs
Fr. Henry C. Gonzalez - Smoke Inhal. Treated at scene - R&R 2 hrs.
Fr. James D. Rogers - Smoke Inhal., Heat Ex., Cut Face - Treated at scene - ML 2 days
Fr. Philip J. Frial - Smoke Inhal., Heat Ex. - Treated at scene - ML 2 days
Fr. Edward [illegible] - Smoke Inhal., Heat Ex. - Treated at scene - ML 2 days
Fr. Ronald J. McGhee - Smoke Inhal., Heat Ex. Treated at scene - ML 1 day
Fr. Robert [illegible] - Smoke Inhal., Heat Ex. Treated at scene - ML 2 days

Respectfully submitted

Paul H. Geidel

Lieutenant, Rescue Co. 1 Gr. 13

This 2nd Avenue disaster was the largest loss of telephone service, approximately 300,000 circuits and 10 cellphone towers, which occurred from a fire that was ever reported in United States history. The media focused on the fire, the loss of service and the difficulties of repairing the damage and returning service. However, the true story was the terrible health issues, cancers and loss of life sustained by the 699 FDNY firefighters many years after. History will never be accurate because of the many firefighters who retired and there was never any further contact.

FINAL

DAILY NEWS

NEW YORK'S PICTURE NEWSPAPER

15¢

FUMES FELL 217 IN PHONE FIRE

Service to 170,000 Shut Off

E. Side Blaze Rages 17 Hrs.

House Votes $21B Tax Cut

44

CHALLENGE

August 20, 1958

I was first appointed to Ladder Company 10 on February 1, 1957 in lower Manhattan as a probationary firefighter. There wasn't much fire duty in this area so our skills were developed with constant drills. I can remember there was a period of time when we didn't turn a wheel for over 60 days. Ladder 10 was a 1941, seventy-five foot Seagrave, with a rear tiller, which enabled us to get through tight city streets in the area.

I can remember a challenge was made to the chief in charge that Ladder 10 was able to ladder a building faster then the new American LaFrance hydraulic truck that Ladder Company 1 was issued. The chief immediately took up the challenge and ordered both Ladder 10 and Ladder 1 to take a position side by side in front of Ladder 1's firehouse on Duane Street.

Down the block across from one another were two four story buildings. The chief took a stance between the two ladder companies and said, "When I give the order "GO" you both respond down the street and ladder the building on your side."

Hence, the chief gave the order, "GO".

Immediately, both rigs responded with Ladder 1 arriving first in front of the buildings. Ladder 10 quickly behind. Everyone scurrying about doing their assigned tasks. Ladder 10's tiller man removed the steering wheel and seat giving the ladder clearance when released. Tormenters, (outriggers) were set for both ladders at the same time. Ladder 10's chauffer released the spring loaded ladder while others raised the fly ladder extension. Another wheel positioned the ladder facing the building. Ladder 1 used their hydraulic controls which brought their ladder around facing the building and at the same time raised their fly ladder. The speed of L-10's spring loaded release was a far greater speed than Ladder 1's hydraulic ladder. Ladder 10 quickly laddered their building first.

There were many arguments after that test. However, it took all five of Ladder 10's men to do this operation and Ladder 1 only needed two firefighters.

45

MY FIREFIGHTING CAREER WASN'T OVER YET

1976

After fighting fires for twenty years it was time to retire. Not that I wanted it to end, but after falling down a staircase at a fire in the New York Times building my career ended. I was devastated! However, things happen for a reason and what was to be, was to be. I was young and knew that I still had plenty of life in me to seek work.

Rescue Co. 1
requests the honor of your presence
at the Annual Dinner Dance
in honor of
Lt. Paul Geidel
upon his retirement from
The New York City Fire Dept.
November 5, 1977
Cocktail Hour 8 to 9
Dinner 9 to 1
Hotel Lexington
Lexington Avenue and 48th Street

One of my hobbies, wood-working, could become my full time job. So, I decided to venture into home improvements and build kitchen cabinets and furniture. My home basement shop was over eleven hundred square feet which had a range of various tools that covered just about every project.

I advertised in a penny saver paper which was all I needed to get started on my new full-time job. I built custom-made kitchen counter tops; Formica and solid surface granite. I became so skilled with making Formica kitchen counter tops, that I was able to call myself a professional.

The year of my retirement 1976 was hectic, very busy. I divorced my wife of seventeen years. However, we had four beautiful children together.

Three boys and a girl. My boys are Gary Paul Geidel the oldest, Ralph William Geidel second oldest, Michael G. Geidel, fourth in line and my daughter Christine Ann Geidel, third oldest.

The boys all became New York City firefighters and my daughter, who graduated from Wagner College on Staten Island, became a scientist with Schering Plough, currently employed at Merck & Co., Inc.

Gary and Michael were assigned to Rescue Company 1 in Manhattan, New York and Ralph was assigned to Engine Company 225 in Brooklyn, New York.

I retired from Rescue Company 1 at the end of November 1976. I became a grandfather for the first time on December 17th with Ralph Geidel Jr. and I lost my dad on December 21st 1976. It was a lot to process that year.

Twenty five years flew by quickly since my retirement. I met my new love Barbara Ann and after seventeen years of dating, married on August 6th, 1998.

On September 10, 2001, my beautiful wife, Barbara and I were on a cross country trip to visit my son Ralph who lived in Seiad Valley, California. Ralph had a line of duty injury at a fire and was retired shortly afterward. Eventually, he retired to California.

Our trip was carefully planned. We would leave Staten Island and visit Niagara Falls, continue on into Canada, Drive west, then drop down into Michigan, continuing on to Seiad Valley, California.

9-11-2001

While traveling through Canada we decided about four in the afternoon to stop at a local delicatessen near Toronto and pick up some cold cuts and water. While inside the delicatessen, a woman behind the counter asked us where we were from. I replied we were from New York City. She then asks, "What do you think of the Twin Towers crashing to the ground?" I thought she was talking about a movie or something. I didn't know what she was talking about. I had no idea what was going on.

She calmly explained that two jet airliners had crashed into the Twin Towers setting them on fire. People were leaping to their deaths. Then sometime after, both towers had collapsed to the ground.

While traveling we were listening to books on tape and never turned on the radio all day. We had no idea what had happened during our journey.

Immediate panic hit my gut. I knew Rescue Company 1 was there. I also knew this was bad, real bad and prayed Mike and Gary were both off that day.

We immediately ran to the car and turned on the radio. Almost every station was reporting the news of the Twin Towers collapsing.

I called Gary and Michael on my cell phone and received no answer. I called my daughter Christine and got through to my son-in-law, Paul Norris. Most phone lines were busy, but thankfully I got to talk to him.

He said, "I heard from Michael and not Gary." We talked a few minutes and my wife Barbara and I headed back home to Staten Island. About an hour later we learned that Gary was called into work for an overtime tour. He was off, but getting ready to retire, so he grabbed any overtime he could to build up his pension. I was sick to my stomach.

We were lucky getting back across the border into the states without a problem. However, we were so very tired and stopped at a motel to get some sleep. Once in the motel we turned on the television and for the first time we saw the towers ablaze than come crashing down. I knew from experience there would be few survivors. I felt helpless and sick inside. I worried about Gary and the rest of the members of Rescue Company 1. I worried about all those poor souls.

I couldn't sleep so we got back into the car and continued driving until we got home.

The next day I suited up in my old firefighting turnout gear. After getting information where to go from Fire Department Headquarters, I went to Marine Company 9, the fireboat assigned on Staten Island. About one hundred off-duty and volunteer firefighters boarded the boat and rode it from Staten Island to Manhattan.

Once there and at Ground Zero I immediately worked on the bucket brigade for about three hours.

Later, I located members of Rescue Company 1 and together continued search for any possible survivors. Gary and ten other members of my old company were missing.

For the next eight and a half months I worked at Ground Zero with my two sons, Ralph and Michael along with my son- in-law, Paul Norris, bringing people home. Below is a photo, from left to right, my son Michael, me, and my son Ralph.

Photo at Ground Zero during the recovery operation, left to right, my son Firefighter Michael Geidel, my daughter Christine Norris, me, and my son, retired firefighter, Ralph Geidel. Christine was able to gain access to Ground Zero because she was dressed in firefighter's gear. She wanted to be part of the recovery looking for her older brother Gary.

Eight members of Rescue Company 1 were recovered early on. Three members were still missing. Gary was one of the missing. Photo below is what remained of Rescue Company 1 after the towers collapsed.

During the next eight and a half months I attended scores of firefighter funerals and memorials.

The end of May 2002, I attended the closing of Ground Zero.

Pictured left to right, son-in-law Paul Norris, Recovery worker Ronda Villamia, me, recovery worker Denise Villamia, Firefighter Ralph Geidel. Our work there had ended. We swept the footprints of the former World Trade Center clean. My son Gary's remains were never recovered. Photo below show the footprints of the World Trade Center.

On August 22, 2002 my son Gary's memorial was held at Sailors Snug Harbor, Staten Island, New York. Thousands were in attendance. It was a hot summer day with a clear blue sky above. I was proud to lead the memorial procession. Gary's empty coffin was being carried on top of fire engine.

Gary, a former U.S. Marine received a twenty-one gun salute and a Marine helicopter fly over.

In the nearby water way, the fireboat, Firefighter, gave a red, white and blue water display in his honor. Mayor Gulliani, as well as Mayor Bloomberg were in attendance.

Gary's mother Patricia was also in attendance and gave a beautiful eulogy about our precious son.

As a result of breathing in toxins over the period of eight and a half months at Ground Zero, my son, Ralph became ill. On October 22, 2014 he died, joining his brother Gary in heaven. We had a Celebration of Life for Ralph at my home in Henderson, Nevada. Ralph was a former U.S Marine, just like his brother Gary and he also received a twenty one gun salute.

Photos of Ralph below -during the recovery at Ground Zero.

THANK YOU

I want to give a special thank you to my wonderful wife, Barbara Ann for helping me so often with spelling structure and editing. Also for keeping away from me during many hours of story writings.

A special thank you to Gary Solomon in guiding me and putting together this book and his patience with me. It has been a long road trying to remember so many years of the past.

Thank you Sharon Geidel, my daughter-in-law for all the time she put in editing my stories.

Gary Suson, thank you for being my friend and writing the forward for my book.